Foundations of Great Storytelling

Preparing to Write

G.C. Boris

M. Haskell

FOUNDATIONS OF GREAT STORYTELLING: PREPARING TO WRITE

An Omnibus of Genre, Novel Planning, Productivity & Author Career Strategy Guides for Writers

ISBN (Paperback) 978-0-9994354-9-6

Cover Design by Fresh Design

First edition. September 2023

Introduction

When we first started writing, we had no idea what we were doing. Consequently, it was incredibly difficult to plan a project or schedule outside help. How long would it take to write 80,000 words? *No clue*. How much time did we need for polishing and editing? *Shrug*. The process felt like a never-ending tunnel. It could be suffocating. Sometimes we'd find ourselves depressed at the thought of all the work ahead.

However, after about twenty books between the two of us, we have a better idea of the steps needed for pre-writing, first drafting, editing, and all the other stages involved in the production of a book. So, who are we and why are we writing this quick guide?

Megan Haskell is an award winning fantasy author. Greta Boris is a USA Today Bestselling mystery author. Together we are The Author Wheel. We began our teaching relationship a number of years ago when we realized how differently we ran our author lives. It was an 'aha' moment for us both.

There is no single correct way to produce, publish, or promote a book.

Introduction

This revelation got our wheels turning. What if we taught courses from different points of view? For instance, Megan is focused on time-saving techniques because she has children at home. Greta is more concerned with managing her schedule and motivation because she doesn't. Megan always wanted to run her own publishing imprint. Greta wanted a traditional publishing deal. Megan is a discovery writer. Greta is a recovering plotter.

We believe by joining forces we're able to address more issues, come up with more creative solutions, and challenge our readers and students, as well as ourselves, to try new things. Whether your goal is to write one book or a hundred, becoming an author isn't an easy process. We still occasionally feel swamped by our to-do list, but something we both agree on is that the best way to combat the overwhelm is to break things down into the smallest pieces possible.

Thus began our journey toward Foundations of Great Storytelling: Preparing to Write.

In this omnibus guide we will provide a bird's eye view of the path to becoming a professional author.

We start with productive writing habits, providing you with tools, tips, and tricks that will help you forge a writing process that will work for you and your lifestyle. Then we get into genre: what is it and why do you care? In part three, we talk about creativity, research, and planning for your fictional world. And in the final section we'll help you build an author career strategy that will help you chart a path toward success—as *you* define it.

Writing is a solitary endeavor. Whether you have a pending deadline or you're only responsible to yourself, the work of crafting a story begins between your fingers and the keyboard. However, it doesn't end there.

Although this book isn't terribly long, it is absolutely

Introduction

packed with actionable information you can use *today* to move your writing forward.

We suggest you take your time with each section and each chapter. Think through your process, needs, and skills. Apply the recommendations that work for you, try something new, and ignore the advice that doesn't fit.

Our goal is to cut through the overwhelm, so you can keep your stories rolling.

Part One
Understanding Genre

Chapter 1
What is genre and why is it important?

As we said in the introduction, when we began writing novels, we still had a lot to learn about writing and publishing. We knew we loved reading and stories and storytelling, but we didn't think of books in terms of genre. There were simply books we loved and books we didn't. Of course, we knew the difference between a fantasy story and a murder mystery, but we didn't understand the rules and subtleties within those genres.

Most writers are readers first, and enthusiastic readers often enjoy all kinds of books. It's not unusual for someone's first manuscript to be a mash-up of all the genres they love to read. While blending science fiction and western, romance and murder, or fantasy and noir has brought about some exciting new subgenres, the authors who penned those books understood what they were doing. They took an educated risk, and it worked.

The first book Greta pitched didn't. An agent told her the manuscript read like a thriller in some places, romantic suspense in others, and had a literary tone that wouldn't sit well with genre readers. Her suggestion was for Greta to pick one thing and do it. Problem was, Greta thought she had. She thought she'd written a thriller.

This is an all too familiar story. New writers often get so carried away by their initial ideas and the thrill of creativity, they crash through literary boundaries that have been erected for a reason. It's a conundrum. How do we write something publishers will consider and readers will love, yet allow our creative brains free rein? The simple answer is timing.

All Megan's stories begin with the spark of a character. The hero usually arrives in an image, a fragment of a scene. In the book she's currently writing, the protagonist is a twenty-something descendant of the pre-biblical spirit of Lilith. She appeared in Megan's mind as a server in a diner, serving an elderly woman who does something magical, gives Lilith some sort of blessing or power, and then promptly dies.

Greta's first novel grew from a string of words: *Apathy began at her head and oozed down her body like a fungus.* Who was this woman? Why all the oozing apathy? Greta wrote the book to find out. Other novels have sprung from news stories, bits of history, or strange ideas she's run across.

Perhaps you've had a similar experience. A vivid dream, a weird situation in a friend's life, something you read online, or a fictional character captivated you and wouldn't let go. That's artistic inspiration, and it's wonderful. These embers are fabulous starting points.

However, we've learned that if we don't want our characters wandering around for pages and pages, lost and confused, we must get the logical side of our brains involved. Before we start the hard work of putting words on the page, we need to know what we're writing. What type of story are we trying to tell? What kind of reader are we going to target? Even writers of literary fiction–the artsy stuff–need to have a plan.

When Greta was writing the third book in her *Seven*

Deadly Sins Murders series, she had what she thought was a fantastic idea. A woman needed to die outside her protagonist's window from a disease that rarely kills people today. For reasons she's never been able to explain, Greta decided to kill her poor victim with Bubonic plague.

She spent several weeks researching and taking extensive notes on the disease. She met with a law enforcement professional to find out how the CDC would handle a modern case of the black plague. After reading two books and an untold number of online articles, she felt ready to write.

About 10,000 words in, Greta's progress came to a screeching halt. The story had gotten incredibly complex. She had to introduce characters from governmental agencies, extend her timeline because of quarantines and explore various political issues. When she complained about the problem, her husband asked, "Does it have to be the plague?"

No. It didn't!

It could've been TB, measles, or any number of diseases that rarely kill today. The sickness itself wasn't a central point of the plot. At least, it shouldn't have been. But the black death is terrifying. It's mythical in its horror and it took over the novel. It became the antagonist.

If Greta wanted to write a medical thriller, it would have been perfect. But this book was supposed to be psychological suspense. By choosing the wrong illness, she changed the genre of her book and wasted a ton of time.

So what exactly is genre?

The word comes from the French for "kind" or "sort." Genre can be defined by the combination of subject matter, tone, length and/or technique. Today, we often define it as the shelf your book would appear on in the library, bookstore, or online retailer. Would they house your title with literary

5

fiction, historical, young adult, or mystery? The answer is your genre.

Think of genre as a tree with a split trunk. One part is fiction. The other nonfiction. If you're writing a memoir or some other fact-based book, that's nonfiction. If you're writing something from your imagination, it's fiction. Simple, right?

Well, it would be, but each trunk has multiple large branches, and those branches host mid-sized branches. The mid-sized branches have smaller branches growing out from them, and the smaller branches sometimes sprout tiny twigs of distinction.

Since we're discussing novel writing in this book, we'll concentrate on the fictional side of the tree. You're probably familiar with most of its larger branches. These include (but aren't limited to) fantasy, horror, historical, literary or general, crime, romance, science, family epics and young adult.

Each of these genres has a particular set of what are called story tropes. According to YourDictionary.com, a story trope is *a common convention in a particular medium. It refers to anything that gets used often enough to be recognized.* Examples are: a bad guy wearing a black hat in a western, a locked room puzzle in a murder mystery, and enemies becoming lovers in a romance.

New writers sometimes confuse tropes with clichés, and while that is one definition of the term, it isn't what we are addressing here. If you've been beating yourself up because you can't think of something that's never been done, something completely original, give yourself a break. There is nothing new under the sun. Even if there was, readers wouldn't buy it. Especially not from a new author. Familiarity with a twist is what most readers crave.

Seasoned writers use tropes like artists use color. They know readers expect certain elements in specific types of novels. These elements can include setting, character types, pacing, voice, themes, objects, animals, and more. Your choice of tropes, the way you combine and present them, is where artistic expression comes into play.

In *The Shining*, for example, Stephen King added realism to the haunted house trope when he introduced an abusive husband, a device more common in psychological suspense. He paired the familiar with a twist and was wildly successful in doing it.

The tropes you choose often dictate your genre. For example, many thrillers have a literal or figurative ticking-clock. A bomb will explode if the hero doesn't disarm it in time. Or the love interest will be killed if the protagonist, a retired thief, doesn't steal and bring a museum artifact to the villain by a certain deadline.

However, many kinds of stories can employ a ticking-clock trope. If your hero is a gun-slinging cowboy and the bomb is on a runaway train, you have a western. If the protagonist thief uses magic to break into the museum where the oil lamp everyone believes to be a simple artifact (but actually houses a djinn) is being kept, you have a fantasy.

As you can see, certain settings or elements take precedence when attempting to define genre. It can be confusing. No wonder many writers struggle to place labels on their stories. And it gets worse.

There are subgenres.

Let's take the fantasy branch of the literary tree to illustrate this. Within fantasy, there's epic fantasy, sword & sorcery, paranormal romance, urban fantasy, time-travel, young adult, and more. Each of these subgenres has a particular common combination of tropes that defines it.

Epic fantasy, for instance, typically involves a secondary (non-earth) world with cross-cultural conflict. The stakes are world changing. There are often multiple point of view characters, and the story may involve a quest across a broad landscape or travel between kingdoms. Lord of the Rings is a classic example of epic fantasy.

Urban fantasy, however, must take place in a city on a modern earth. Normal humans are often (although not always) unaware of the magic in the world. The stakes may be world changing, but they're not political (i.e.: not two governments going to war), and the story typically focuses on a single protagonist who must solve a mystery or uncover a truth. The Dresden Files by Jim Butcher are a good example of urban fantasy.

Although every broad genre breaks down into smaller subgenres, subgenres aren't necessarily used to classify books in physical libraries or bookstores. If you walk into Barnes and Noble, you'll find psychological suspense and medical thrillers in the same section, so Greta has some excuse for her confusion. However, the online stores—which have unlimited shelf space—are different. They can be very granular in their categorization.

Why? Why not simply call a romance a romance, or a thriller a thriller? Why drive writers nuts with all these categories? Won't this genre thing stunt my creativity?

The answer is multifaceted. Let's look at it from the reader's point of view first. Most have specific tastes. Rhonda may love romance, but she wants it sweet. Steamy bedroom scenes aren't her thing. Martin may enjoy mysteries, but doesn't appreciate talking cats that help the protagonist solve the crimes. The quicker and easier it is for a reader to understand the experience they'll get from a title, the happier they'll be.

There are advantages for authors, too. Not only does understanding genre distinctions help us write more targeted stories, but from a marketing point of view, sending a clear message about your book makes it easier to find readers who will enjoy it. This means fewer negative reviews and more true fans.

Hopefully, we've convinced you that getting a grip on your genre is worth your time. In the next chapter, we'll tell you how to do it.

Activity:

1. Consider your story idea. What is the top-level genre of your story?
2. Spend a few minutes traveling the "genre tree" on Amazon:

- From the home page, click on Kindle eBooks near the top of the page, below the search bar.
- Next look at the left sidebar and scroll down to the "Department" categories. Click on your genre.
- Keep clicking on narrower genres to see the books that are listed in each niche subgenre.
- Consider where your book idea might fit!

Chapter 2
How to Discover Your Story's Genre

I n our book, *PUBLISH: Take Charge of Your Author Career*, and its companion course, *Self-publish or get an agent? How to find and implement your best path to publishing success,* we encourage our students to do the following exercise to understand their genre as they develop their path to publication. However, it's even better to do this research *before* you write your book for reasons we'll go over in the next chapter. But wherever you are on the journey, grab a yellow pad and a pen and dive into the following exercise.

Step 1: Make a List

Do an online search to find books similar to the one you've written or hope to write. Make a list of at least ten bestsellers and/or award-winning books published in the past two to three years.

You may not find something exactly like your book, so don't get hung up on minor issues here. If you think your book is a mystery but it also has a time-travel component, choose mysteries with fantastical elements. Maybe their sleuth can read minds or talk to ghosts. Or maybe you find a historical mystery set in the same time period your hero travels to. That's close enough. The novels you target won't have all the same tropes as yours.

Now, take this list and your legal pad and head to your local library. If you don't have access to a physical library, you can use Amazon as your virtual library. Find as many of those titles as possible and bring them to a table (real or virtual). If you're doing the work on a site like Amazon, we suggest downloading samples for each of the titles you're planning to research.

Step 2: Take Notes

Answer the following questions about each of the books. (You can download a worksheet for this exercise in the links at the end of this guide.)

What genre and subgenres does the book fall into?

You can find this information in the product details at an online retail store. Libraries list the subgenre in the online catalog, and it will show at least the broad genre category on the physical book's spine.

What are the titles?

Identify similarities in length, wording, and themes in each of the titles. We all remember the thriller "Girl" books from a few years back. Often, you'll see a trend.

How long are these books?

Jot down how many pages each has. Also, look at the chapters. How many are there? Are they long or short or varied lengths?

This is a bit more difficult to assess on Amazon unless you buy the books, but you can at least see the first few chapters and find the total page number in the product details. Having said that, buying the books isn't a bad idea. Keeping up with the bestsellers in our genre is part of the job.

What's the point of view?

Are the stories in first person? Third person close or distant? How many POV (point of view) characters does it have?

Again, each book may not be the same, but you'll often notice a trend. Young adult stories, for example, are almost always in the first person with one protagonist. International thrillers tend to have several point-of-view characters who speak in third-person close.

What is the writing style?

This question is more subjective. We suggest you look at things like the length of the words and sentences. Does the language seem casual—words we normally use in everyday speech—or is it more formal? Is there a lot of white space on the page, or is it a sea of ink? Does the author include long descriptions of setting and people? Is there a lot of dialogue?

Certain genres tend toward certain tenses as well. Are the ones you're researching written in past tense, present tense, or some of both? Suspense novels, for instance, often switch tenses as they tell two plot lines—one in the past, one in the present—that eventually merge.

What are the main plot points and tropes?

For this we suggest reading the book synopsis on the back covers or the sales pages, especially if you haven't actually read the novels. Again, you'll begin to see patterns.

The popularity of certain tropes comes and goes. *Twilight* brought on a rash of paranormal romances for young adults. *Gone Girl* made unreliable narrators popular in psychological thrillers. Note where the stories intersect.

How do the books open?

Read the first couple of pages. How does the author hook the reader? Do they dive right into the story, or edge you in slowly? Is there a prologue, or does it start with the primary character? How soon does the inciting incident appear?

Is the book a standalone novel, or is it part of a series?

This is a critical question that we'll be addressing further in Chapter 5. Readers expect a series in certain genres, and there are different types of series. If your goal is to be a career writer, often it's good to tackle one of these genres. However, there's nothing wrong with writing a standalone novel or two to get your feet wet.

Step 3: Decision Making

Once you finish your research, you should have a pretty good idea of where your book fits in the bookstore, or how you should label it if you plan to pitch to agents or editors.

But wait, there's more! Understanding your novel's genre will not only assist you in selling it but also in writing and revising it. As we've said, readers come to the genre table with certain expectations. If you'd like to skip the embarrassment Greta experienced when pitching that first novel she now refers to as her Frankenstein book—too many genres sloppily stitched together—read on.

Activity:

1. Grab a pad of paper and a pen, or join our community to download the Know Your Genre Exercise at www.authorwheel.com/foundations.
2. Find at least ten books similar to yours that are either bestsellers or award winners.
3. Go to your local library or look on Amazon to answer the questions in this chapter.

Chapter 3
Using Genre to Craft Your Story

From the previous chapters, it may sound as if we're promoting the concept of *Writing to Market*. While we think that's often a smart and savvy approach, it isn't what we're suggesting here. Nor do we do it in its purest form.

If you're unfamiliar with the term, writing to market is when an author studies the particular tropes that are currently selling in a particular genre and writes that book. For instance, billionaire romances were hot several years ago. Many romance authors noticed, wrote books with billionaire romantic leads, and made—if not a billion—a bundle.

Some authors saw the trend and developed a story to fit, starting from scratch. Others may have already had an idea that could be tweaked to fit the billionaire romance tropes. Either way, that's not what this chapter is about. Instead, it's about educating yourself on your specific market to make sure your book fits the broad outlines, not fine tuning it to mimic current trends.

Think of it this way: in order to play a musical instrument, people need to know their scales, the differences between major and minor, diminished and augmented, etc. The more skilled the musician, the more advanced their knowledge of music theory will be. Genre tropes, archetypes, and story structure are parts of writing theory, like chord structure is part of music theory. It all works together to form a harmonious whole.

We each have a unique voice and want to tell a unique story. And we should. That's what makes writing and reading enjoyable. If all stories were the same, why would we write another? Our point is, parameters are really, really helpful. Understanding the basics allows us to create something new and unexpected that still satisfies reader preferences.

Is there a marketing element in this? Sure. If you're penning a story for fun or posterity, none of this stuff matters. If you're hoping to sell books, it does. However, we believe understanding your genre is about more than sales. It's also about writing a book that readers will enjoy.

Having said all that, it's time to apply what we've learned from Chapter 2 to our writing. Let's dig in and create our own personal style guide.

Length

When we start a new novel, we both use Scrivener to get organized. However, any word processing software will work. It's a method Greta learned from Melissa Storm's course Writing and Marketing the Cozy Mystery.

This process is significantly easier when we know approximately how long we want our stories to be and how many chapters they should have. For example, based on the genre research from the prior chapter, we know that if we're writing a classic epic fantasy, our book is going to be at least 150k words, which we'll divide into approximately 60 chapters. If we're writing a contemporary fantasy adventure, we'll need to write about 80k words and 40 chapters.

Let's pretend you're writing the contemporary fantasy adventure mentioned above. If you're in Scrivener, simply start a new project and create 40 empty folders—one for each chapter. If you're using Word, or a similar program, start a book folder, then create 40 chapter documents within that.

To set your word count goals for each chapter, divide the book's length by the number of chapters. For example, an 80k word book divided by 40 chapters gives you a goal of approximately 2,000 words per chapter. In Scrivener, you can set this up as a daily writing goal. In Word, you'll just have to keep track.

Greta—who's more of a plotter than Megan—likes to give as many of her chapters titles and descriptions as possible. This provides a rough outline of her novel. Megan, on the other hand, prefers to leave them as basic numbers, only filling in the few plot points she has in mind where she thinks they might go.

When you do this, you may discover you have tons of ideas for the end of the book, but the middle is hazy. Or maybe you know how the book opens, but you have no idea how it will end. That's fine. You can brainstorm new plot points, or discovery-write your way through. Either way, having the empty folders or documents and word count targets gives you a visual representation of the work ahead. And you'll always know how far you are from The End.

If your story is already written and it's way off track in length, you'll need to edit heavily, or flesh it out. We suggest you set up the chapters as explained above, then copy and paste your work into the correct folder or document. This experiment will show you immediately where your manuscript needs work.

If your story is too short, do you need to add chapters? Or maybe you need to lengthen the chapters you've already written. If the book is too long, you may find that while most of your chapters are approximately 2,000 words, there are a couple of sections that need serious trimming.

Point of View

Next, based on your notes, what perspective will your target readers expect? As a rule of thumb, novels with several point-of-view characters will be in the third person. Stories told by only one character can be either first person or third person. It's an artistic decision.

Geo-political thrillers often have many point-of-view characters. Consequently, they're told in third person. Romance novels are typically written in close third person because they switch points of view between the hero and heroine from chapter to chapter. Smaller scale stories like contemporary or urban fantasy, suburban suspense, and young adult novels are often in first person.

Point of view is an important decision. It's no fun to rewrite an entire novel to change it. Knowing what's acceptable in your genre early on will help you frame your story in a way that makes the most sense for your reader.

Can you color outside the lines and write an epic fantasy from first person or an omniscient action-adventure? Sure. But the conventions exist for a reason. In the first case, the reader may find it hard to sit inside only one character's thoughts for 500 pages. In the second, an omniscient narrator distances the reader from the action.

However, you may find that in your chosen genre, the narrators are all over the board. If so, you'll need to decide which character or characters will best tell the story. Greta's *Seven Deadly Sins Murders* series has multiple points of view, most of which are in third person. However, she and her editor decided early-on that in each story there would be one character who would remain anonymous for most of the book. Often it was the antagonist. This was her way of bringing the *Who Done it?* trope into her psychological suspense.

That character, they discovered, had to speak in first person. It was almost impossible to have them speak in third person, like the rest of the characters, without revealing their identity. Because Greta found a handful of bestselling thrillers that included both third-person characters and first-person characters in the same novel, she knew she was safe.

The Girl on the Train also broke the first person/third person rule. That book has several POV characters who are all represented in first person. Paula Hawkins, the author, included the character name at the start of every chapter to delineate who was speaking. Some readers loved this. Some hated it. Obviously, it was a risk that succeeded for her.

The bottom line is, you don't have to follow the genre norms. But it's wise to know what they are, why they exist, and have a valid reason for deviating from them if you do.

Style

One reason we both read lots of books in our respective genres is because style isn't easy to pin down. Like the judge said when asked to define pornography, "I can't give you a definition, but I know it when I see it."

There is a tremendous difference between Stephen King's writing style and Dean Koontz's, although both are considered masters of the thriller and horror genres. However, here are a few things that may help you analyze style and create your own.

How do the characters think and speak?

For example, historical fiction will need to match the language and tone of its era—modernizations can turn off readers. Megan once received a negative review for using the word "okay" in a fantasy set in a non-earth realm with a medieval vibe. However, a political thriller can and probably should use modern slang and colloquialisms. Keep in mind the main character's personality as well. Some genres lend themselves really well to snarky cynicism and witty dialogue, while others look for calm logic.

Dialogue vs. Action vs. Exposition

Readers want a balance of dialogue, action, and exposition, but not all readers desire the same balance. Short, action-oriented books generally only have enough description to ground readers in the setting. Contemporary romance uses a lot of dialogue to develop relationships between characters. Science-fiction books, especially space operas, have detailed explanations of the science behind the futuristic machines and settings.

Pacing, or how fast or slow a story moves.

Again, different genres have different paces, but how do writers achieve that? Here are a few tips:

Up the stakes to up the pace. Less time between action sequences creates a faster read. You can amp up the adrenaline with a tense, life-or-death scene, or by foreshadowing the big battle to come. Keep reminding the reader what's at stake.

More white space on the page decreases reading time, thus quickens the pace. Dialogue can help with that. Especially quippy back-and-forths.

Description and exposition slow the pace. Long sentences

and long paragraphs fill the page with text which lengthens reading time. This is perfect for a more thoughtful, literary story, an epic quest, or even used judiciously in a thrill ride to give your readers a break.

Word choice matters. This goes back to our discussion on voice, but it affects pacing as well. Multisyllabic words, especially ones your readers may not be familiar with, can slow things down. Shorter sentences with shorter words increase the pace.

Tense can increase the tension. Present tense feels, well, more present. Past tense implies the action has already taken place. Subliminally, your reader knows if your protagonist is telling the story in the past tense, they didn't die before the end. It's a small tension reliever, but it is one. Some novels, especially those that move back and forth between time periods, will use both present and past tenses, creating a balancing act.

Plots and Tropes

Finally, when the research is done, you're better able to make informed decisions about which tropes you're going to use, which you're going to twist to your own purpose, and which you're going to leave behind. You can dial in the details of your story idea to meet the reader's expectations and then use that information to build an audience eager for your story.

One thing Greta learned early in her writing career was that the day of the swooning heroine waiting for her hero to rescue her was dead. While that used to be a common thriller trope, readers no longer wanted a passive female lead. She had to rewrite the ending of her first book to make her protagonist more proactive in her own rescue. You can be sure, she is now current on which tropes within mystery/thriller are popular and which aren't.

In Megan's case, one trope she's already identified is the setting of her new book. It's a modern-day, small city which she knows fits well with the new adult, contemporary, fantasy subgenre. Reading several novels in that subgenre has helped her decide which story lines to pursue and which won't work before she's married to any of them. As an added bonus, she knows when it comes time to market, she can target contemporary fantasy, urban fantasy, and paranormal romance if she develops a romantic relationship in the story.

Activity:

1. If you haven't yet written your novel, write down which elements from your research you're going to include in your story. Incorporate those tropes and styles in your outline or notes.
2. If you've already finished the first draft of your novel, go back and re-read the story with these elements in mind. Have you met your readers' expectations? If not, what might you tweak to better match your subgenre?

Chapter 4
The Pros and Cons of Switching Genres

As we mentioned at the beginning of this book, writers are readers first. As a reader, you probably enjoy many genres, and that's great. The more widely you read, the more interesting your books will be. Not only that, but writing in multiple genres may be the only way to fill your creative well.

However, it isn't always the best strategy from a marketing perspective. The disadvantages are pretty obvious. It's time and labor intensive to grow an audience. The more genres you write in, the more reader groups you must appeal to. The people who enjoy your sci-fi novel aren't the target market for your young adult romance series.

If you write in two or more genres and use the same author name, you risk confusing your readers. Cynthia loves your cozy cat mysteries. She sees your name on the cover of a book outside that series and assumes it will be similar because, after all, it's you. Imagine how upset she'll be when she discovers it's a steamy reverse-harem romance novel.

The common fix for this problem is to create a new pen name, but this is where the time and labor come into play. For every pen name you use, you must replicate your platform building. Each name should have its own website, mailing list, social media sites, etc. Make sure you're committed before heading down this path.

If the new genre won't offend or upset your current reader base, you don't have to hide the pen name. The names can even be closely related. For instance, Joanna Penn of The Creative Penn podcast uses Joanna Penn for her nonfiction work and J.F. Penn for her fiction novels. Since she targets her nonfiction to the writing community, it's interesting for those in the business to see what else she's doing.

However, taking the example of cozy mysteries and steamy romances above, that author would risk alienating their various bases with their other work. They would need to do their best to hide or at least completely separate their reader groups.

So, what can you do if you don't have the time or energy to manage a separate pen name, but your muse won't work if you stick with one genre? Here are a couple of ideas:

Hire someone to run the pen name

We know, we know. When you're starting out, you don't have a lot of money to burn. However, if you get really organized, you may be able to afford a virtual assistant to pass on the time-consuming parts of the job to, like updating your website and social media pages, and managing your email list. If you're making the creative decisions, this might work for you.

Pitch agents and publishing houses

Many hybrid authors publish one series or type of book on their own and another with a publisher. While they still have to maintain more than one website, social media persona and email list, they're saving time on the publishing aspects of the job.

Traditionally published authors may find that their publisher and/or agent have an opinion about whether it's a good idea to start a pen name. Their contract might even specify the "right of first refusal"—meaning the publisher chooses whether they want to purchase the rights to a new book before the author can pursue other opportunities.

Best-selling or high-earning authors may find their publisher more than willing to sign an alter ego or work with the author on a marketing plan that makes sense. If not, it could be back to the query trenches.

Write in an adjacent genre

Some writers successfully segue from one subgenre to a related one. For instance, Nora Roberts writes contemporary romance, romantic suspense, and supernatural stories with strong romantic elements. Not all of her readers will like all three, but they are similar enough to create crossover.

However, it's worth noting that she writes murder mysteries under a completely different pen name, J.D. Robb, because they appeal to a completely different reader. Even a superstar like Nora Roberts is cautious about mixing up her audiences.

If you choose to write in adjacent genres under the same name, it's a good idea to separate them with careful branding. For instance, Greta has a psychological suspense series and a paranormal mystery series. All the books fall under the mystery-thriller heading, so they're adjacent genres.

Still, some readers won't enjoy both, so the covers are distinctly different. The psychological covers are more artistic and serious. They are built around a single image and don't have a person on the cover. The paranormal covers are darker, less serious, and include a model. Also, the series names and logos are prominent on the book covers.

Create a co-writing team

Another tactic to consider is writing with another author. Having two names on the cover signals to readers that the book is different from what each author might write on their own. The two names together become a kind of pen name.

James Patterson has created a literary empire with this tactic. His first books to hit bestseller lists were thrillers, and he stuck to that genre for many years. When he branched out, he took on other writers. Now he oversees the writing of children's books, young adult books, romances, and almost every crime subgenre you can think of. He produces a staggering number of titles a year because he's only doing a fraction of the work.

As you may have noticed, we're big on the idea of learning from other people's mistakes and successes. If you're thinking of jumping the genre fence, see if you can find a popular author who writes in the multiple genres you want to write in. It may take some digging, especially if they're not open about their second pen name.

When you find one, note how they're handling the situation. Consider signing up for both of their email lists if they have them. Follow them on all their social media platforms. What are they doing that makes sense to you? Is there anything you can replicate? What rubs you the wrong way or overwhelms you? This information could be a starting point for your own business plan.

Activity:

1. Write down the pros and cons of starting a project in a new genre. Consider the cost in time and money as well as the benefits of creative freedom. Is it worth it?
2. If you decide to start a project in a new genre, consider the best method of managing reader expectations. Do you need to start a pen name? Does it need to be secret? How can you leverage help from other people to achieve your goals?

Chapter 5
Writing a Series

Once upon a time there was a writer who got a great idea. She planned to write a loosely linked series of standalone books all set in the same world with many of the same characters and tie them together by theme—the Seven Deadly Sins. We wish we could say she wrote them with joy and ease and lived happily ever after.

Greta is, of course, the protagonist of this story. She found a publisher for the series, so it was a pretty good idea. And as you know, if you read our bios, she's already written the final book. However, there was plenty of angst and pencil chewing along the way.

One thing we say on the homepage of our website is: *Between us, we have over 20 years of writing and publishing experience. We've made the mistakes, so you don't have to.*

In this chapter, Greta will share the three biggest mistakes she made when writing *The Seven Deadly Sins Murders* series. Before we jump into that, however, let's define the various types of series.

Greta took a class from romance author Lisa Wells on this subject. According to Ms. Wells, there are four basic types: the really big book, the linked sequential, the linked standalone, and the loosely connected standalone.

An example of the really big book series is the *Lord of the Rings* trilogy by J.R.R. Tolkien. Book one begins Frodo's story, book two continues it and book three wraps it up. If it wouldn't break your arm to hold, the entire trilogy could be one really big book.

Jan Karon's *Mitford* series is an example of a linked sequential series. In this series, there is an overarching storyline that moves from book to book. Read out of order, you might wonder who certain characters are and when so and so got married. However, each novel has a complete plot and a satisfying conclusion at its end.

The linked standalone series is the most popular of the mystery and crime genres. Think Agatha Christie's *Miss Marple Mysteries*, or Lee Child's *Jack Reacher* series. Each story is complete. We can read them out of order without feeling like we missed something. What links them is the protagonist.

Finally, there are the loosely connected standalone novels. In these, each story is complete and has its own protagonist. What connects them is the world and cast of characters. An example of this is Tana French's *Dublin Murder Squad* books. All her protagonists work for the Irish Murder Squad. Each story is a separate case, solved by its own detective, but she connects the stories through the world she has created.

Certain genres lend themselves to certain types of series. Fantasy, especially high fantasy, is perfect for the big book because often the author is telling the story of a world, or an epic journey with a huge cast of characters. It's a history of sorts.

The linked sequential series naturally follows a character through the stages of life, or a family through the generations.

Linked standalone novels are a perfect foil for the quirky detective. Loosely connected standalone series work really well in romance where a cast of characters each have their turn leading a story.

Greta wanted to write domestic suspense, and by definition domestic suspense occurs when something bizarre happens to Joe Blow Average. The plots revolve around a normal person—not a cop, or an ex-Navy Seal, or a crime reporter—who stumbles into a life or death situation. It wouldn't be realistic for a real estate agent, a librarian, or a home chef to run into dead bodies every month, so each book had to have a different protagonist. The loosely connected standalone type of series was the solution.

That's what Greta did right. Now, onto her mistakes.

Mistake #1:

Greta was so excited about starting her first book, she didn't consider how to roll out the series. She thought the only thing she needed to know before she started typing was the plot of the book she was currently writing and her continuity rules, which were:

- Each story would take place in Orange County, California
- Each story would feature a different female protagonist
- The protagonist for the next book would appear in the previous book
- There would be a character who spoke in first person who would remain a mystery for at least part of the novel

- Each book would explore the theme of the title sin in unexpected ways

What else did she need?

Greta didn't realize that series, like single titles, have an arc. Or they should. Half-way through book three, *The Sanctity of Sloth*, she realized the stories were taking on a more philosophical tone. That was fine, but if she wanted to wax more philosophical, she should have had *A Pinch of Gluttony* appear earlier in the series. It's hard to be completely serious about gluttony. For some reason, it's a funnier sin. Who knew?

Solution

Consider the arc of your series before you begin. Even in a series of standalone novels, you will have a starting point, a midpoint, and an endpoint. Think about the journey you want to bring your readers on. Do you want to hook them with thrills and chills, take them gradually into a darker place, then return them to a happier world at the end? Plan your line-up carefully.

Mistake #2:

Greta never considered the amount and type of information she would give away from book to book. Writers must be careful about what their characters say, especially when writing mystery-suspense. Characters can be gossipy. For example, if the protagonist of book two is friendly with the protagonist of book one, that means she knows the resolution of book one's mystery. Since Greta's stories can be read out of order, she couldn't allow her current hero to spill the beans.

On the flip side, if the characters say nothing about the

events of the earlier novels, it's not realistic. If Rosie was almost killed in book four and her best friend never acknowledges that in book five, it makes the fictional world seem very two dimensional.

Solution:

Again, plan, plan, plan. During the plotting phases of each individual story, highlight the characters who know what happened in prior books. List the things they can and can't say. Think about where you'll fit those conversations and how you'll end them if they're heading toward spoilers.

Greta had to have a character in *The Key of Greed* collapse in the middle of a conversation in order to interrupt her protagonist before she said too much about *A Pinch of Gluttony*. It was a close call!

Mistake #3

When Greta began the Sins, she never thought about teasing the next book at the end of the one she was writing. This was a big mistake, especially since she was writing standalone books. Why should a reader follow through? What would draw them onward to the next in series?

Another problem that occurs from this lack of forethought is that character jobs, love interests, and settings may be published before you write the next book. What if none of those things work for your future storyline?

Too bad.

Greta often had to make things work in ways that were much more difficult than they would've been if she'd thought about the series as a whole before she sent her first manuscript off to the publisher.

Solution

Plot the next in series at least partially before you end your current manuscript. Know roughly what the characters are going to do, even if you don't know all the details. Your writing life will be easier, and you'll be able to add a few teasers into the final pages to create curiosity about what will happen next.

Many industry pros believe it's easier to create a fan base with a series than with a standalone story. If you've already written a novel, it might be worth considering its series potential. Try taking a hard look at your book. Can you spin off it? Is it long enough to divide into three books? Or could your next book, like Tolkien's *The Hobbit*, be a prequel to a series?

Think about writing a series if they're common in your market. If they aren't, how can you twist the common tropes to include one?

Whether you're starting your first novel or tenth, rewriting a book, or plotting the next five, set yourself up for greater success by understanding your genre.

Activity:

1. Are series common in your genre? If so, what kind of series is most appropriate?
2. Does your book have series potential? Write down some ideas for continuing the story or creating spin-offs to expand your fictional world.

Part Two
Planning a Novel

Chapter 6
Feed Your Creativity

I f you ask ten writers what they do before they begin a new project, most will tell you about the research they're doing or their favorite plotting tool. They may also mention story beats and character development.

That's good. All these things are necessary for a solid story foundation. However, there's one thing that's often overlooked: the care and feeding of your creative brain. You've heard it said, you are what you eat. Nutrition is essential to health. Similarly, brain food—both quality and quantity—will affect your creative output.

Input

If you write, you need to read, and it's especially good to read the genre you want to write. This is Fiction Author 101. It may sound obvious, but we've actually run into a surprising number of people who try to write without being readers first.

We devour novels. Traditionally published and independent authors, bestsellers and sleepers, old books from deceased writers and this year's award winners, we read it all and allow those stories to permeate our minds and feed our writing muscles. It can be time-consuming, but it's part of the job. We heartily recommend audio books for those who can't sit still after a long day at the computer.

We also watch movies and TV series. This can be very educational because screenwriters must accomplish everything in a fraction of the time it takes to read a book. A viewer can experience a full story arc in an hour and a half rather than the eight or ten hours it takes to read a novel. It's a great way to see the big picture without getting lost in the weeds.

However, if you only watch and never read the written word, we doubt you'll be able to write novels well. We've both been called upon to read new writers' material at conferences and in workshops. Sorry to say, we can tell if they're not readers. Although both films and books are forms of storytelling, their creation requires separate skill sets.

Education

Books, courses, and workshops on writing craft are another way to feed our creative brains. While we don't believe an MFA in Creative Writing is necessary to turn out a decent novel, learning from those who've gone before is essential.

A basic understanding of any industry is required to work within it. If you're going to sell houses, you'd better know the local market, current interest rates, what it takes to get a loan, and so on. If you're going to write and sell books, you'll need to have a handle on popular genres and their tropes, story structure, character development, and pacing, just to name a few among other things. It is much easier to learn that information from someone else than to parse it out on your own.

To see if your efforts are hitting the mark, critique groups can also be a great resource. We go more in-depth about critique groups in our book *PUBLISH - Take Charge of Your*

Author Career. But for those not sure of what we're talking about, a critique group is a group of writers who meet either in-person or online and agree to provide constructive feedback on each other's work.

The structure of the feedback depends on the group. Some like to read pages in advance so that the reader has time to make thoughtful suggestions before responding. Sometimes the responses are written on the page, like an old-school editor. Other groups like to have the writer read their work in front of the room and provide verbal feedback immediately. Often there are rules about proper etiquette in the group and critique procedures.

Greta's group, Fictionaires, has been around for fifty years. The group comprises mostly experienced, published (or soon-to-be-published) writers in a wide variety of genres. They meet every other week. Two to three writers will read selections of their work-in-progress while the rest listen and make notes. They then circle the table offering helpful criticism to the one who read. Whether you're the reader or the listener, there's always something to be learned from the other members of the group. This kind of positive, experienced environment will quickly improve a writer's craft.

However, a bad critique group can make things worse. If the group is mocking or demeaning, pick up your notebook and leave. Personal attacks and intentionally nasty comments are unnecessary and only discourage your efforts. Don't let them. Pay attention to the spirit in which they offer the critique and find a group that will offer positive feedback and encouragement alongside the helpful criticism.

On the flip side, some critique groups turn into mutual admiration societies whose work nobody outside the group enjoys. This is a more common occurrence if you've skipped the first requirement: a diverse experience level. If everyone is a beginner, they might not know how to be critical. Alternatively, if everyone is too worried about hurting your feelings to tell you what's wrong, you may get a false sense that your work is ready when it's not.

Writer's Block

Everything we've mentioned so far is good nutrition for your creative brain. However, just as junk food undermines a healthy diet, negativity and self-doubt are poison to creativity. A quote that would be funny if it wasn't so often true goes something like this:

Give a person a book, and they'll be entertained for a night. Give them a writing career, and they'll have crippling insecurity for life.

Insecurity is a creativity killer. It comes in many forms. One of the most prevalent for authors is imposter syndrome. This is the internal sense that even when by many standards we are successful, we feel like we're actually frauds.

There's a comic that depicts two business people seated at a desk with a cockroach. The thought bubble over the bug's head reads, "I wonder when they're going to realize I'm a cockroach." That's imposter syndrome in a nutshell.

It can come when we meet a goal, like publishing a book launch or signing a contract with a publisher. We may, at first, feel happy or excited, but then we start to question our own success. Maybe we think we don't really deserve it. Or we compare ourselves to someone else and feel like even though we met our goal, it's not good enough. Maybe we didn't hit our sales targets, or we doubt we'll be able to maintain the momentum and publish the next book as quickly as some other author. Unchecked, imposter syndrome can lead to writer's block.

Some people say writer's block is an imaginary infirmity, an excuse for laziness. But we've both experienced mild forms of it, and we're here to tell you, it's real. The symptoms vary, but can range from an inability to focus to full-on depression accompanied by drug or alcohol abuse.

If you're experiencing something like the far extreme we've just described, stop, put this book down, and call your doctor. If you're in emotional distress or considering self-harm and located in the US, please call 988, the National Suicide Prevention Hotline.

Your health is much more important than your ability to write or not write a story.

However, if you're only smarting from the little twinges we all feel from time to time, read on.

Rejection, whether it comes as an email from an agent or a one star review from a reader, is never fun. If you are pitching stories to industry professionals, you will receive rejections. It's just a fact. More than seventy agents and editors rejected Greta's manuscript before she found her publisher. This is difficult for even the most confident writers. We suggest doing your best to gamify the process.

Set a target number of queries to send per week. Chart the responses on a spreadsheet. Each time you get a "no, thank you," rejoice that they bothered to respond at all. If they gave you feedback on the query or the manuscript, even better. You're getting closer! Tell yourself this is a numbers game and every "no" is one more person you've eliminated from the pool of possibilities on the way to your "yes."

Another way to handle this process is to network. Go to conferences, meet with agents, and get their feedback on your work. Even if that specific agent doesn't want to represent you (which may have nothing to do with your writing), they might suggest a different agent or publisher that is a better fit for your book.

You can also set a time limit. When Greta was pitching her first series, she gave herself one year. At the end of that time, if she hadn't found an agent or a publisher, she was going to publish independently. A publisher bought her series about a month before the end of that year.

Megan never sought a traditional publishing deal, but that doesn't mean she's never felt the dark side of writing and publishing. Envy of someone else's *overnight* success (which is rarely overnight if the truth were told) leads to self-pity. A book launch that doesn't meet our expectations makes us feel like complete and utter failures. We've each lost hours of productive writing time due to negative emotions.

We've discovered the best way to avoid the crippling insecurity of writer's block is to stop these things before they take hold. You can't keep the birds from flying over your head, but you don't have to allow them to make a nest in your hair.

Here are a few suggestions:

- Don't dwell on a rejection.
- Do <u>write down every success</u>, big or small, and read it when you're feeling low. Met your word count goal for the week? Success. Finished a first draft? Success. Received a positive review? Success!
- Don't read your negative reviews.
- Do read the negative reviews of your favorite famous or classic authors. Steven King and Jane Austen have 1 star reviews, and they can be a good reminder that <u>even the masters have critics</u>.
- Don't attend toxic critique groups. If the critiques get personal, walk away.

- Do <u>find a supportive network</u> of writers whose opinion you trust. The best are those who can help you find your mistakes and grow in your craft, while cheering you on and commiserating with your struggles.
- Don't believe the overnight success stories. (Those writers have been banging the keyboard for years, trust us.)
- Do remind yourself that a writing career is a <u>marathon, not a sprint.</u> Books last practically forever and may find their audience years after they're first published.
- Don't edit your first chapter a hundred times before you finish the book. You'll just have to edit it again when you get to The End.
- Do your best to <u>shut down your internal critic</u> while you're writing your first draft. This will improve your mental "flow" and writing speed, limit the number of edits that will just have to be edited again, and reduce the occurrence of imposter syndrome.
- Don't gossip about other writers. You never know when your own negative words will come back to haunt you.
- Do <u>be happy for other authors</u> when they succeed and cheer them on. Remember that a rising tide raises all boats.
- Don't sit and stare at a blank computer screen for hours on end.
- Do get out and <u>take a walk</u>, get some fresh air, or change the scenery. Sometimes getting the blood pumping or moving to a new location can freshen not only our lungs but also our creative brains.

Most of all, remember that fiction writing is a learned skill. Like anything, it requires practice, patience, and persistence. As writers and creatives, we're on a continuing journey to improve and perfect our craft, with the goal that every book will be better than the last.

Action Steps:

1. Read three books and watch three shows in your genre.
2. Take a course, a workshop, or read a book on an area of writing craft you feel you need to improve on.
3. Write down every writing success you've had, big or small, and post it somewhere near your computer to motivate you.

Chapter 7
Brainstorming

We know none of what we suggested in Chapter 6 sounds onerous. Do what we love—read and watch fiction—and avoid that which makes us miserable. As a result, friends and family often confuse our brain-feeding sessions with entertainment, which to be honest, they are. Hence, writers often get a bad rap for having their heads in the clouds. We're known for ignoring the real world in favor of imaginary lands, but this is precisely what it takes to write fiction.

Which brings us to our next point. There is a difference between simply absorbing fantasy and stepping into a *productive* daydreaming stage. The former can become a sneaky way of procrastinating. The latter is an important part of story development.

Productive Daydreaming

Whether we create a detailed outline before we type chapter one, or we prefer to discover the plot as we go, the subconscious mind is where our stories come from. Some like to call it the muse. Stephen King calls it 'the boys in the basement.'

The words writers use to refer to the process make it sound mysterious, because there is an element of mystery to it. One of the most common questions fiction authors are asked is: Where do you get your ideas? Honestly, much of the time we don't know. No one really understands what goes on in the shadowy recesses of our brains.

However, while we love a good mystery as much as the next person, we also recognize that couching the writing process in those terms makes it feel inaccessible, especially for newer writers. There's no easy answer for where we get our ideas, but there is a process that can help germinate them. We like to call it productive daydreaming.

Demystifying the Muse

Productive daydreaming requires three things: information, time, and trust.

Think of your imagination as a flowerpot full of dirt made from all the books, movies, and TV you've absorbed. Dirt has nutrients necessary for plant growth. But if you don't put seeds into your soil, nothing will grow. So, the next step is to plant something.

Megan writes fantasy based on historic myths. Before she starts a new book or series, she spends a lot of time pondering and researching her germ of an idea. She watches YouTube videos on the myths and legends that apply, reads news articles and encyclopedia entries on the ancient cultures that created them, and studies as much of the original literature as she can find. All these things are seeds from which a story can grow.

Once our seeds are in the soil, we must allow our subconscious to do its job. This can be rough for the control freaks among us. We wish we could tell you how long it will take for your seeds to germinate, but we can't. There isn't a set amount of time like the nine months needed to grow a baby human or the 22 months for an African Bush Elephant. Each story seems to have its own gestational period.

This is where trust comes into play. It's tempting to rip our story seeds out of the pot and examine them for roots before their time. However, this is a surefire way to destroy our fragile seedlings.

Once when Greta was on a deadline, she forged ahead with a novel even though she hadn't allowed all her idea-seeds to blossom into their logical conclusions. As a result, she made a critical mistake part way through the novel. She ended up having to ask her publisher for an extension so she could completely rework the second half of the book. It would've been less time-consuming if she'd allowed herself that extra time on the front end.

Exercise and Rest

The good news is, productive daydreaming can happen while you're doing something else, even finishing your latest book. Some activities actually act like water and fertilizer for your seeds. Repetitive, mindless chores like house cleaning or taking the dog for a walk are excellent for unlocking our subconscious minds.

While we're out in the sunshine hiking or running or kayaking (Greta's favorite new workout) our subconscious is free to mull things over without our conscious mind interfering. We like to micromanage, but our creative self thrives on freedom. Our physical brain also benefits from the increased blood flow and oxygen uptake that happens when we exercise. It's a win-win.

Taking the time to take care of ourselves helps break through creative blocks and boost our productivity. The fact is, if the body stagnates, often so does the mind. It may seem counterintuitive, but by taking extra time to care for our bodies (which may reduce our word count today), we're giving ourselves the chance to write for our whole lives (a higher future total word count.)

We know multiple writers who suffer from injuries or health problems that affect their writing. Carpal tunnel is incredibly common. Back, neck, and shoulder pain are frequent concerns. Pain diminishes our creativity. It can make it hard to think, let alone type.

Meanwhile, movement has been proven to boost creativity. Stanford researchers found[1] that "creative output increased by an average of 60 percent when the person was walking" versus sitting.

We're not healthcare professionals. If you have health concerns, see your doctor. But if you're feeling the effects of writers' block or the need for a creative boost, try to get some movement in your day.

Conversely, some of our most productive daydreaming sessions occur when we're physically resting. As we drift off into that space between sleep and wakefulness the subconscious rises to the surface.

When Megan hits a sticky spot in the plot of her story, she'll sometimes choose to take a daydream break rather than trying to force words on the page. With a notebook and pen in hand, she stretches out on the couch or a comfy chair and preps her mind by contemplating the characters and the current events in the story. Who are they? Why are they in the place they've come to? Who are their enemies, internal and external? Then she closes her eyes and imagines she's in a bubble, or one of those sensory deprivation tanks. She lets her mind wander wherever it wants to go—so long as it's related to the story and not household chores.

Allowing the muse to wander while loosely pondering our stories often yields spectacular results. It's in this place we forge new fictional pathways and make connections that were otherwise unseen.

When good ideas pass through her mind, Megan quickly writes them down in her notebook. Sometimes, that's all she needed to navigate the problem. Other times, she'll return to the dream state to unlock even deeper mental vaults.

Every once in a while, she'll even take an actual nap, only to find the answer she needed when she wakes.

Daydreaming is essential before starting a new story, but this technique also helps anytime we find ourselves stuck at a crossroads, unable to decide where the characters should go next. When this happens, we suggest finding a quiet, comfy spot to close your eyes. It might not look like work, but it can be really productive.

Mind Maps

If you feel that productive daydreaming is a little too woo-woo for you, never fear. Once we sense an actual plot forming in our heads, we pull out the pens and whiteboards and create mind maps.

A mind map is a brainstorming technique that visually connects related ideas. You begin with a single thought (or image) and then branch out from that concept with anything and everything you can think of that relates to that idea. Each new concept can branch out as well, or even circle back to other related ideas, or ultimately move into its own chart.

Megan's latest series began with the idea for a character. Lilith is a woman who can bridge the gap between the mortal Earth world and the spiritual realms. She placed that concept at the center of her map, then started asking questions.

- How many worlds are there?
- How does Lilith get from one to another?
- Did she always have this ability, or how did she come to have it?
- What problems does this cause?
- What happened to the original mythological Lilith?

She could answer these questions because she'd used the productive daydreaming technique mentioned above. Her brain was packed with idea-seedlings.

Each answer became its own circled "node." Some of those answers generated their own questions, which branched off into their own answers, and sometimes branched even farther than that. Pretty soon, Megan had a cloud of information and ideas related to the project.

This is the power of the mind map. It changes our perspective from a linear, chronological format, to a fluffy mass of creativity bound only by our ability to follow our thoughts to new and exciting locales.

Greta uses mind maps differently. Since she writes murder mysteries and thrillers, she begins her maps with a dead body. Her questions are about relationships.

- Who might want to kill Bill?
- Why?
- What is their relationship to him?
- What is their relationship to the other characters?
- How might they do it?

Soon, she has a cloud of potential villains, murder methods, and red herrings along with possible plot twists.

We suggest you move fast through this process and avoid critique. Think of brainstorming as play, rather than test taking.

One reason children are so incredibly creative is because they are solidly devoted to play.

Write things down as fast as you can. If you change your mind midway through you can erase it, so don't get hung up on perfectionism. No one will see this but you. Let the branches flow from one to the next as you explore your ideas.

Megan uses a giant whiteboard for her mind maps. Since she knows she can erase it, she's free to focus on the goal: story development. Once she's finished, erased and rewritten to her heart's content, she takes a picture and files it in a dedicated photo album on her phone. Random ideas scribbled on napkins and receipts also get photographed and filed away. You can see an example of Megan's whiteboard mind maps by clicking here.

Greta, on the other hand, doesn't have a whiteboard. Instead, she uses a looseleaf notebook. She keeps one for each series. These notebooks contain more than just mind maps. She often writes possible synopses, scene ideas, character sketches and backstories, and even draws maps of story locations. These are all powerful methods of brainstorming your novel.

Action Steps:

1. Spend a day or a week or more daydreaming about the story you want to write.
2. Read articles and watch shows with that specific story idea in mind.
3. After giving your brain some time to contemplate all you've read and learned and thought about, try creating a mind map for your story and see where it takes you!

Chapter 8
The Basics of Worldbuilding

Y ou may be tempted to skip this chapter if your story is set in a realistic, modern day world, but don't. Although historical fiction, science fiction, and fantasy arguably require the most worldbuilding, every book needs a solid foundation from which the story can grow.

We'll discuss character creation more in Chapter 9. However, we believe that worldbuilding and character creation go hand in hand. We subscribe to the motto: *Build it and they will come.* Your characters will grow more and more three dimensional along with their environment.

The reverse is true as well. If you don't build your fictional world, your characters will wander in an empty void destined to be mere shadows of what they could have been.

It took Tolkien about 38 years to create Middle Earth. While we don't think you need to spend anywhere near that kind of time on your world, we are saying worldbuilding is not to be overlooked. Unless you're writing some sort of metaphysical exploration of the afterlife, we suggest you avoid the empty void.

Depending on your genre and reader expectations, your worldbuilding may focus on only a few elements, or you may need to tackle many. (Make sure to read the section on Understanding Your Genre if this statement confuses you.)

For example, if you're writing a modern day thriller set in the US, you won't need to spend a lot of time on the creation of a natural world. It's Earth. However, a modern day thriller will still need to be grounded in the geography and culture of its primary setting. New Orleans is distinct from Seattle, which is distinct from Beijing, which is even more different from rural Minnesota. You'll need to be familiar with the areas you write in.

Speculative fiction requires much more worldbuilding than thrillers do since it diverges so strongly from modern reality. To make the magical seem real or the impossible seem plausible, many things will need to be well-established. In this case, the sub-genre rather than the genre will dictate which elements will require the most creativity.

For example, in epic fantasy, you might craft a medieval Earth analogue using the technology and cultural aspects of Europe in that era. In other words, you'll have no guns but lots of castles, swords, and armor. However, you'll need to imagine a landscape for your characters to quest through, establish the kinds of creatures that populate your world, and clarify the magic system.

Urban fantasy, on the other hand, can rely on real-world settings, but you'll still need to invent the species of animals and humanoids and establish the magic rules.

As you can see, even though you've got random bits and pieces of your plot, characters, and setting mind-mapped, you've still got work to do. It's time to create something, but not a novel. Not yet. If you're like us, we know you're eager to get writing, but there are a few more steps before you begin.

There are entire books written on worldbuilding, and we

will recommend one or two in the resources section. But to get you started, we suggest you think through the following.

The Natural World or Setting

This can be as involved as the creation of another planet with different levels of gravity, seasons, lengths of days, and alien life forms. Or it can be as simple as imagining a small town Somewhere, USA.

A group of authors Greta knows decided to each write a romance novel set in the same fictional city. They called it Rancho Allegro, set it in Southern California, and had many long city planning meetings. They named the streets and parks, talked about municipal offices, and decided what kinds of shops that would populate Main Street. That city continues to grow as they write new stories within its boundaries.

Timeframe

The historical fiction writer will have the most work when establishing the timeframe of their world. They have to research everything from clothing to architecture to food and beyond. And because readers of this genre like to nit pick, they'd better get things right. An author we know received a one star review for including potatoes in a fantasy novel set in the middle ages. Apparently potatoes didn't arrive in Europe until the late 1600s. Who knew?

Because of the work involved, many authors of historical fiction choose one place and one time period and stick with them book after book. It's tough enough becoming an expert on Victorian England or Viking culture without repeating the process across a wide gap of time and place.

For writers penning more contemporary novels, decisions

may need to be made about what to *leave out* of their stories. Slang, technology, pop culture, and political happenings will date your book. This means, your novel may seem out of date when those things change.

Greta recently considered building Ring-type video doorbell cameras into a murder mystery. The technology might have made an interesting plot twist, but technology changes quickly. If next year Ring loses popularity and something new comes on the market, it would make her book seem dated. She left it out.

Language and Idioms

Language and idioms are also key to making a story believable. If your character lives in the 1800s but describes herself as a "foodie"—a term that came into vogue because of a New York Times article written in the 1980s—you have a problem.

Everyday expressions like "by and large," "take it with a grain of salt," and "winning hands down" all have history. If your characters are from a past era, you'll need to know which expressions were used in that time period.

Different parts of the world use distinctive speech patterns as well. People from England and America, for instance, often use different words for the same things despite the fact that they all speak English. If your character is a Brit they will not say, "Put the stroller in the trunk." They'll say, "Put the pram in the boot."

You can also create new language, expressions, and names for a fantastical world. These words can make your story feel more real. Muggles, squib, and quidditch from the Harry Potter books have become part of our modern vernacular. This is because they seem so authentic we've adopted them.

Using modern lingo in fantasy or sci-fi settings can sometimes backfire. Megan received a negative review for using the word "okay" in her alternate world fantasy, even though her characters interacted with modern day Earth.

Political and/or Cultural Systems

This is another significant topic for historical writers. They need to research not only the big set pieces like wars, political leaders, and natural disasters of the time, but also the culture.

Who rode in horse-drawn carriages? Who walked? Was there a difference depending on their class or station in life? It was odd that Jane Austen's Elizabeth Bennett liked to walk everywhere, but had she been a servant, it might have been expected.

Those writing contemporary real-world settings will need to decide which cultural or political events will affect their stories. Whether or not to include COVID has been a big topic among authors for the past couple of years.

Are readers tired of thinking about the pandemic? Do they want to escape into a fantasy world where masks and lock-downs don't exist? Or do they want a book that represents what's currently happening? These are the kinds of questions writers grapple with.

Greta included COVID in one of her books without actu-ally naming the disease, because she needed it for a prison break. Apparently, federal penitentiaries sent many inmates to county prisons because of overcrowding during lockdown. It's easier to escape from state and county prisons than from federal ones, something that came in handy for her plot.

Even fantasy and science fiction authors often have to think through the politics of their imaginary worlds. If their plot lines revolve around wars or oppressive governments, the details will need to be ironed out before their characters can react to their circumstances. They must also consider how closely they want fictional events to reflect reality.

Magical Systems

Fantasy authors aren't the only writers who need to work through magic systems. If a book has any futuristic, surreal, paranormal, clairvoyant, or time travel elements, writers need to consider the rules of engagement.

When Greta began her *Mortician Murders* series, she had to decide if her main character only received sensations from the hair of murder victims, or from all dead people. Did she see ghosts? Did they talk to her? How could she get rid of them if they were haunting her? And what did a haunting entail?

Time travel is both a popular and a complicated story element. How much of the future can be altered by a character that visits the past? Can they change world events? Or only those things that affect their family and friends? Do their clothes travel with them, or do they arrive in the past or future naked? How much time elapses while they are out of their own time?

As you can see, there is more than witch's brews, silver bullets, and Vulcan mind melds to consider.

Religion

Religion deserves its own category, although it could fall under culture or magic systems depending on its role in your story.

If an author is writing Christian Fiction, for instance, certain cultural rules will preside over their books. Their characters won't smoke, cuss, or chew, or run around with people who do. Some characters will pray, and often prayers will be answered in miraculous ways. There is always the sense that an omnipresent God is involved from the sidelines.

In fantasy novels, a writer might create a religion from scratch. It may or may not have supernatural power depending on the storyline. *Dune* is a good example of a powerless religion. Herbert's creation was primarily a political tool. C. S. Lewis's *Chronicles of Narnia*, on the other hand, portrays a godlike Aslan who has the ultimate power to right the wrongs of the land.

Science

Science is used in genres other than science fiction. Genuine science can be a jumping off place like in *The Martian* or it can be completely fictional like the spaceships and other technology of *Star Wars*. It can be set on other planets or solar systems, or right here at home in a hospital room. We can find it in horror novels, like *Jaws* by Peter Benchley, or adventure stories, like *The Ice Limit* by Lincoln Child.

Scientific news often inspires novelists to ask themselves, "What if?" Many, if not most, of Michael Crichton's stories from *Andromeda Strain* to *Jurassic Park* came from things that were actually being talked about in the scientific community when he was writing. Medical thrillers use current breakthroughs, medications, or diseases as the starting points of nail-biting stories.

Science in all its forms is a great catalyst for fiction. However, similar to the nit-picky historical fiction readers, those who enjoy their fiction with a bit of science are often armchair scientists. They're the kind of people who subscribe to Scientific America. If your research is sloppy, you'll hear about it.

Final Thoughts on Worldbuilding

Ultimately, reader immersion is the end goal of the fiction writer. The reader should feel part of the story. You want them to become addicted, to be unable to put the book down. You want them to buy the next book before they've even finished the first.

This means you don't want to do anything that will pull them out of your world or interrupt their reading experience. Unfortunately, it's almost impossible to know *exactly* what will cause that interruption.

If your reader is an expert in a subject, and you write a minor detail wrong, they might shut the book for the night, or worse, shut it for good.

But don't lose hope. We're not writing for that one individual. We're writing for a larger audience. If you focus on creating a complete and consistent world, most readers will stay onboard.

Action Step:

Think through all the elements mentioned in this chapter and decide which are pertinent to your story. Make a list of topics to research.

Chapter 9
Research

N ow that you have the basic components of strong world-building in your head, it's time to apply them to your specific project. This means research.

To show you how we start this process, we'll use Megan's latest novel as an example.

Aether Bound is a contemporary fantasy with a twenty-something protagonist who can see the spiritual influences affecting people. The angel or demon on their shoulder, so to speak. Here's the rough shape of her world:

The natural world or setting - There will be two realms in this universe, the Seen and the Unseen, also known as Earth and Aether. The Seen is modern day Earth, primarily set in the US. The Unseen is the realm of the gods and spirits.

Research:

- The real world city the Seen takes place in.
- The pantheon of gods and their minions, including mythological creatures, and boundaries and designs dictated by the gods who live in the Unseen.

Magic System - Lilith will have several magical abilities, including the ability to see and converse with spirits, travel between the realms, and manipulate spiritual connections.

Research:

- The myths surrounding the historic Lilith, seeing spirits and/or traveling between realms.

Religion - Megan is incorporating gods and religions as far back as Ancient Mesopotamia.

Research:

- The gods and deities needed for each story in the series.

You can see how each of the elements above interplays with the others. The selection of a god to include in a story will impact the history, culture, and technology of that particular Unseen kingdom.

Choosing the city or town where Lilith lives in the Seen realm will affect the specific technologies and culture she encounters and deals with every day. If she's in a big city, she'll have skyscrapers and traffic. If she's in a rural town, she'll have small-town gossips and interactions with wildlife.

Research Methods

Now that we understand what we should research, let's discuss how we do it. We use three ways to tackle the process depending on the thing we need to know and how we're going to use the information.

The first is the traditional approach. Let's say you decide to set your book at the Ritz Carlton in New York. You've never been there, so you pull up Google Earth and look at the building and the neighborhood surrounding the Ritz. Next, you read about the hotel on their website to understand their policies and perks. Maybe you take a virtual tour of the rooms. You've found what you need for your story, no more, no less.

The second approach is what we call immersion. In the book Greta is currently writing, she needed to create a religion. It couldn't be too serious, or too much like a known religion. She didn't want to offend anyone, but she wanted it to have some roots in reality. She discovered there have been several "Heathen" cults in recent years based on Norse mythology. That sounded like fun.

This time her research was very open-ended. She read anything that sounded interesting to her. Any links, stories, or vocabulary she thought she might want to reference went into a research document. She pumped up her brain with Viking versions of the afterlife, their methods of worship, and attitudes toward morality. Once the pump was primed, she began to write. She allowed that information to emerge organically and color her story as she wrote.

The third form of research is experiential. Say you're writing about an adventure that takes place on a Colorado River canoe trip. In order to write believably about it, you decide you must actually experience it. So, you book a trip. Writer's Police Academy conferences are popular with those who want to shoot a gun, work with a police dog or go on a virtual reality drug bust.

All three forms of research have value. The traditional approach is the least time-consuming, leaving you more time for writing. When you're not sure what you need to know, the immersion approach puts lots of information at your fingertips, and it stimulates creativity. And experiential research helps create more believable sensory detail because you've actually been there and done that.

Beware the Procrastination Trap

We need to give you a note of caution about research. Sometimes writers use it to procrastinate. You would never do that, we're sure, but many people do.

One time Greta spent an entire writing session trying to find out what color the tables were in Santa Ana Jail's visiting room. Why? What difference did it make?

None. That's what. Several months later she asked a retired law enforcement friend. He'd been in that room countless numbers of times. He wrinkled up his brow and thought about it for a long moment. Finally, he said, "I don't remember. White, maybe?"

When we're feeling insecure, or just stuck on a plot point, it's tempting to over-research our story details. We may feel that if we just knew exactly what kind of gun our character was shooting, what bullets it takes, and the manufacturer's history we'd be back on track. To know if this is true, simply ask yourself: Will this information change the plot? If the answer is no, you're spinning your wheels.

Action Step:

Take the list of worldbuilding elements pertaining to your story that you made in the last chapter, choose your research method for each, and do it.

Chapter 10
Standalone or a Series?

I f you spend many months or even years on worldbuilding, you may want to use that world over and over again. And why not? We've all heard that series sell—at least to readers. Sometimes agents and publishers are less enthused if they're talking to an untested author, but that's a topic for another book. We also know that some genres lend themselves well to series writing and readers of those books expect a sequel or two.

However, even if the book you're pondering begs for a sequel, and you've done your research well and ironed out all the details of your fictional world, there are a few more things to consider. First, if a single main character leads the series, is your protagonist fit to carry more than one book? Second, if not, what type of series do you want to write?

Greta wrote a series of standalone novels (*The Seven Deadly Sins Murders*) before she tackled a protagonist-led series because she hadn't yet imagined a character interesting enough to pull off seven books.

There are many ways to develop characters, and we'll go into that in more depth in a future Quick Guide. However, a book on prewriting wouldn't be complete without at least talking about protagonists. So, how do you know if your main character has legs? Here's our checklist.

Are they believable?

Even if you're writing a wizard-vampire or shape-shifting alien, there must be something about your character that seems believable. The Enneagram, a personality-typing method that has been around for centuries, is a fantastic tool to help with this. (There's a link to that website in the resources section of the book.)

There are nine basic Enneagram personality types. We are each only one type, but we have friends and relatives who are others. If you choose one and make sure your character doesn't deviate from that model, they will feel like someone your reader knows.

For instance, if your protagonist is a Type Five Investigator—one of the nine personality types—you wouldn't have them react to a situation the way a Type Two Helper would. Helpers have a distinct set of motivations, fears, and desires.

However, even if you don't use the Enneagram to shape your characters' personalities, they have to remain consistent in their motivations and behaviors. Readers might not be able to articulate the reason, but a character who veers off their personality path won't resonate.

Do they have a past?

Although our characters are born on the page, it shouldn't seem as if they were. Give them a history, and they will be more compelling. Anne of Green Gables was sympathetic because we knew she'd lived in an orphanage before Mathew Cuthbert brought her home. That knowledge triggered our sympathies, which encouraged us to root for her.

Michael Connelly's Harry Bosch has starred in 21 novels and a TV series. Why? Because he's so much more than a hard-nosed cop. His tragic childhood not only colors the way he tackles cases, it also becomes a mysterious thread that is doled out to the reader in short segments as the books progress.

Are they relatable?

We may not want to read about someone just like us, but we don't want to read about someone we have nothing in common with either. We may not be brilliant or cold and calculating, but we like our creature comforts, and we have hobbies. Sherlock Holmes loves his pipe and finds comfort in the violin. Ah, a connection.

Cozy mysteries draw readers in with this concept. We don't solve murders, but we love to knit or cook or eat cheese or drink tea or . . . fill in the blank. Amazon even has a special sub-category of mysteries devoted to crafts and hobbies.

Are they interesting?

We've often heard a character must be likable, but the runaway success of *Gone Girl* disproves that. Amy Dunne, the main character, is anything but likable. However, she *is* interesting. She's the inspiration for her mother's bestselling children's books and that has made her a bit crazy. She's a train wreck we can't look away from.

No matter how creative you are, not everyone is going to be interested in your character. However, the more questions a reader has about them, the more likely that reader will stick with the series.

Megan's newest character, Lil, is a descendant of the mythical Lilith. Lilith was the first wife of Adam or the original she-demon or both depending on the legend you ascribe to. Now, that's just interesting right there. It raises a ton of questions. What happened to the first Lilith? What powers did she have and how were they passed on to her descendants? How many of them are there? Are they really evil? And that's just for starters.

If you develop these aspects of your main character, you'll have a winner even if you don't plan to write a trilogy around them. If you've written a series that doesn't center on one protagonist, remember there's more than one kind of series. (If you need a refresher on the series types, go back and re-read Chapter 5.)

Action Steps:

1. Review the Enneagram Institute website and see if one of the personality types can be applied to your character(s).
2. For your protagonist and each of the significant characters, ask the following questions:

- What elements of their past influence their present state?
- What elements of their personality or interests make them relatable to readers?
- Are your characters likable? Are they interesting?

3. Consider your series potential:

- Do readers of your genre prefer a series?
- What kinds of series are common in your genre?
- What kind of series might you want to write?

Chapter 11
The Story Bible

A story bible is a document or collection of documents used as a shorthand reference for the details of your book. They can be minimalistic or complex, online or in print, color coded or in simple black and white. But what good story or series bibles all have in common is that they are thorough, easily accessible, and can be shared (maybe even updated!) by others.

The reason we bring this up now, here, in the planning stage is because once again, we want you to learn from our mistakes.

It's so much easier to create a story bible from the very beginning of the idea generation process than it is to create one three books down the road. We've also found that a story bible can help us organize our thoughts and ideas and research before, during, and after plotting and drafting our novels.

So let's consider what a good story bible looks like.

Thorough

Just as with worldbuilding and research, some authors go crazy with their bibles. They color code, paste in images, and include their main character's entire history and family tree. If you need those things, great. However, since our goal as writers is to write, the less time you spend creating something no one but you, and possibly your editor, is ever going to see, the better.

On the other end of the spectrum, some writers (we're not naming names . . . ahem, naïve young Megan) don't bother making a story bible at all because it takes too much time. These are the folks that don't enjoy scrapbooking or drawing or making to-do lists. They also believe they can keep all their fictional details in their heads.

We've learned the hard way, that while it doesn't have to be a work of art, we need something. We've both spent far too much time scouring past books in our series because we couldn't remember a side character's name or our protagonist's favorite restaurant or the way we spelled danceathon. Was it danceathon, dance-athon, or dance-a-thon? Gah! It'll drive you crazy.

Another crazy-making thing is timelines. When we don't keep track of the calendar, our characters can end up in two places at once, or the wrong age in a future scene, or in a month that has six weeks. All these things have happened to us or to writers we know.

These are the story bible non-negotiables as far as we are concerned:

- Character names and brief descriptions. (It's a bummer when you change a character's eye color halfway through a book and never notice.) Personality types and single-sentence story arcs for the major characters can also be helpful.
- Favorite weapons or objects that they use frequently and consistently. If the weapon has a name, list it.

- Any pets or animals that appear frequently.
- Major settings—description and relevant details that are mentioned in the book.
- Time period (if relevant).
- Any organizations, governmental agencies, or company names that the protagonist interacts with.
- A timeline of your story.
- A glossary of unusual words, fictional words, or expressions your characters use regularly and the way you spell them (i.e. danceathon.)

You might also include your worldbuilding notes. If you've created a magic system, relied on certain scientific facts, or invented a religion, a section on each of these could be helpful.

Easily Accessible

Some authors like to create a notebook with dividers for each of the above categories. Others keep their bibles online in Dropbox, iCloud or Google Docs. Some include it in a special file on their hard drive in the word processing program they're using to write their story. The key is to think about how you'll be using your bible. Here are the pros and cons to the various types of story bibles:

A Paper Bible

Pros

- It's fun to make, decorate, and can be visually pleasing.
- It doesn't require an internet connection.
- It can grow with your book or series.

Cons

- It's more time-consuming to create.
- You must switch from computer to pencil when you update it.
- You have to carry them with you when you write away from home.
- Spreadsheets are limited in size and scope.
- It's not shareable.
- You could lose it or misplace it.

A Writing Software Bible

Pros

- It's stored with the book or books it relates to.
- You don't need an internet connection to access it.
- You can use any kind of document your word processing software provides.

Cons

- It can be difficult to switch back and forth from your manuscript to the bible depending on the software you use.
- If your computer goes down, you'll lose it unless it's backed up.
- It's not shareable.
- It's not tactile if that's something you enjoy.

Megan has tried a few different methods of creating a series bible over the years. For *The Sanyare Chronicles*, she hired her editor to create a bible for her after book three, when she finally realized she needed it. The editor put everything in Word, which worked, but felt clunky because it wasn't stored with her in-progress writing as she was working on the fourth book in the series.

Older and wiser now, Megan is creating the bible as she writes each book in *The Rise of Lilith* series. She writes in Scrivener, and the software has a built-in folder system that allows for research, setting descriptions, and character profiles to be kept in the same project with the manuscript. As an added benefit, Scrivener is accessible across all devices via Dropbox (including desktop, laptop, and mobile devices), can be accessed offline, and syncs whenever internet is available.

The drawback, however, is that it's not easily shareable with a third party, which is why Greta prefers the Online Bible method.

Online Bible (Dropbox, iCloud, Google Docs, etc)

Pros

- It's accessible anywhere as long as you have an internet connection.
- You can designate a folder and add as many files to it as you want.
- You can store any kind of document or image.
- You can share it with your publisher or editor.

Cons

- If you write in places without an internet connection, you're out of luck.
- It's not tactile if that's something you enjoy.

Greta creates a folder in Google Docs with separate pages for the non-negotiables mentioned above. She opens any pages she may need before she begins writing, then she updates or references those pages as she goes. Her calendar is a spreadsheet. Since she only plots small sections of her book at a time, she can puzzle out her timeline in advance and refer to it as she writes. If the plot changes, it's easy to alter.

Shareable

One of the biggest advantages to keeping your story bible online is that it's shareable. If you're writing your first book, this may not seem important. However, if that book goes to an editor or becomes the first in a series, it will become important.

Giving editors access to your bible can save them—and you—a lot of time. If, for instance, you have a side character named Carol and in one chapter you spell it Carrol and in another Carole and in another Carol, your editor can check the bible and correct the misspellings without having to question you about it. Greta's editor will even make a correction or addition to her bible if she catches something Greta missed.

For writers collaborating on a story with a co-author, having a shareable bible might be essential. Like the romance writers working on a series in a shared world, it's a lot easier to keep everything updated if everyone has immediate access to the story bible.

The point is, while writing a book is generally a solitary endeavor, publishing it isn't. Whether you publish traditionally or independently, you'll eventually work with a team. If that team might benefit from a shared bible, make sure you have a way to keep it updated and in sync.

Action Step:

Choose a method and create a story bible.

Part Three
Productive Writing Habits

Chapter 12
Understanding the Writing Process

Have you ever pondered doing a home-improvement project yourself instead of paying a pro? Greta's husband decided to renovate their kitchen–no small task. He guesstimated it would take him a month to six weeks. It was *six months* before the kitchen was finally complete. What was the problem? His inexperience in construction prevented him from understanding the full complexity and scope of the project.

Each phase of book creation employs a unique process. What works in one phase may not work in another. This is a major reason new writers (and even experienced ones) struggle with goal setting. If you don't have a good grasp of the tasks involved, and how long each will take, it's very difficult to set a timeline for completion.

Another thing Greta's husband didn't take into consideration was that he didn't have complete control of all processes. For instance, the company that cut and installed the granite counter postponed several times before actually showing up. Because the counter wasn't in, he couldn't install the sink or put up the backsplash. Production got pushed down the road.

The good news about writing goals is that you are in charge.

Until you send that book to a critique group, beta readers, or an editor, the whole enchilada is in your hands. Barring illness, hurricanes, or fires, you're in control.

The *bad* news about writing goals is that you are in charge. There's no one to blame if you don't achieve them. However, we believe that having productive writing habits is a combination of understanding the processes, evaluating your strengths and weaknesses with honesty, and trial and error. So, let's get started.

Phase One:

Phase one of novel writing is all about planning. Some buzz words used in writing circles for this stage of the game are world-building and pre-writing. The time needed for these processes depends on what you're planning to write, how long you've been noodling around with your topic, and how much research is needed. It can take anywhere from a week to a year. We go into more detail in our section on Planning Your Novel, but for now, just be aware you'll have to set time related goals for this phase before you begin pounding the keyboard.

We suggest a goal of a certain number of hours per day for a certain number of days. For instance, once you've isolated the tasks you need to do, you might schedule three hours a day for ten days to complete them.

Tasks in this phase may include:

- Researching plot points, settings, and characters' careers
- Researching genre expectations
- World-building

- Sketching out ideas for subsequent books if you're planning a series
- Creating character sheets
- Creating a plot guideline (Whether this is a detailed outline, or a lightly sketched concept is up to you.)
- Setting up your word processing files

Phase Two:

Phase two is the first draft. Goal setting for this is pretty straightforward because it's easily quantified in a daily or weekly word count.

In our experience, most people have long-term goals that are too small, but short-term goals that are almost impossible to achieve. It's better to start easy, gain confidence, succeed, and then exceed.

We believe in a daily (or almost daily) writing habit, however, some people work better in bursts. For the former, we recommend a daily word count goal, and for the latter, weekly.

Regardless, consistency will be key to developing a strong writing habit. If you can sit down in the same place at the same time each day or each week, you'll train your brain to see that time as writing time. And if you start small, with micro-goals that are almost impossible not to achieve, then you'll get the benefit of positive reinforcement.

Your micro-goal may be as low as 50 words. Anyone can write 50 words, right? When you're done, you're done. You've met your goal for the day. Of course, you can write more if you want to, but you've *accomplished what you set out to do.* You're building a habit.

As you improve and gain skill, your daily or weekly goals will naturally increase. We each average between 1,500 and

2,000 words per day when writing a first draft, but we didn't start there. And there are more experienced writers accomplishing more.

As you build your writing habit, you may find some days are easier than others. However, even on hard days, it's good to strive for that minimum word count. Once your micro-goal is an established habit, you can add a target goal and a stretch goal.

For example, when working on a first draft, Megan has a 500 word micro-goal. If that's all she gets in a day, she's not excited, but she's satisfied that she's making forward progress. It keeps the writing habit going, and she doesn't lose the thread of the story between writing sessions.

However, her target goal is 1,500 words per weekday—a number that feels both achievable and productive. For her style of writing, this is usually about the length of one scene, which provides a satisfying conclusion to the writing day.

Then there are the days where the words just flow, and everything feels amazing. On these days, she sets a stretch goal of 2,000 words. Like training a muscle, progressively writing more on some days with easier days in between builds creative capacity and endurance.

Once you've set a realistic micro-goal or target goal, do the math to figure out your completion date. For example, at 2,000 words a day, it will take approximately 40 working days to finish an 80,000 word rough draft. We suggest you give yourself a margin of a week or two to account for the illnesses, floods, and fires mentioned earlier. When you do this, you have a "deadline" to hold yourself accountable to.

Phase Three:

Phase three is the self-editing stage. It's difficult to break this down into word counts. You may need to write a whole new chapter one day, but other days, you'll simply be reading and shifting things around. Two common ways to set goals in this phase are by concept and by chapters.

We both self-edit by concept. For instance, we will do a read-through stage that may take two days. Then, address the plot holes we discovered while reading for another two days. We might fix a flat character arc on day five, and so on.

If you choose this method, it's best to decide on the stages you plan to tackle and in which order. It could look something like this:

- Read cover to cover and take notes - two days
- Fix plot holes and up the tension - three days
- Smooth character motivations and reactions for primary characters - two days for protagonist, a half day for each side character
- Work on settings and sensory details - one day
- Look for overused words and fix awkward language - one day
- Run the manuscript through an editing software program - two days

Other people set a certain number of chapters per day as their goal. Although chapter two might be a mess that takes three days to sort out, they may fly through chapters four through eight in an afternoon. Because things here often average out, a goal of a chapter or two a day can work. A person would simply divide their time by the number of chapters in the book to set that goal. For instance, when editing thirty chapters at an average of two chapters a day, they'd need 15 days to edit the manuscript.

Phase Four:

Phase four is production. This is where things can get really complicated. In fact, we have an entire full-length book and course on the topic. Since this book focuses on writing–not publishing–habits, we'll stop right here.

Activity:

1. Using our examples above, take some time to write out your personal list of tasks for each phase of the fiction writing process.
2. Set an impossible <u>not</u> to achieve daily or weekly micro-goal for your first draft writing phase.

Chapter 13
Setting S.M.A.R.T. Goals

Writing—novel writing in particular—is typically a solitary endeavor, especially in the beginning. Traditionally published authors may have editors or agents imposing deadlines on their work, but more often than not, our only deadlines are our own. In this environment, it can be extremely difficult to create productive writing habits and motivate ourselves to work.

We are creative people. It's the nature of the job. We build worlds and make up stories to entertain our readers. The traits that make us good at our profession can also lead us down wandering paths of distraction, or encourage us to wait for inspiration to strike before sitting down at the keyboard. Unfortunately, these behaviors are not great for getting things done.

In this chapter, we're going to show you how to set realistic goals using the SMART goal setting framework. We've chosen this framework because A) Greta used to be a fitness professional and used this method to help her clients achieve their physical dreams, and B) because it's a well-researched, well-proven system.

SMART goals are:

Specific • **M**easurable • **A**ttainable • **R**ealistic • **T**ime-bound

This system can apply to any set of goals, but for our purposes, we'll focus on the intention to complete a manuscript.

Written goals are forty-two percent more likely to be achieved than unwritten goals[1], according to a study by Dr. Gail Matthews, a psychology professor at the Dominican University in California, so we suggest you grab a pen and paper and start jotting things down.

Specific:

Let's begin with the "S" in SMART. Unless your goals are specific, how can you plan appropriately? How do you know when you've accomplished what you need to accomplish? *I want to write a book* is a vague goal. How about tightening that up?

Examples of Specific Writing Goals:

- Develop the fictional world for my novel - working title
- Finish the first draft of my manuscript
- Revise my manuscript

Measurable:

Now that you've written a specific goal, let's make sure it's measurable. Measurable goals have distinct parameters. For instance, in the world of fitness, your specific goal might be to run a race. To make that goal measurable, you'd say, I want to run a 5K. Now you know how to train.

Examples of Specific and Measurable Writing Goals:

- Research the settings and themes of my novel
- Finish the first draft of a 70,000 word manuscript
- Revise my 35 chapter book

Attainable:

The attainable aspect of goal setting is often where things get confusing. Tasks we've never done before can seem impossible to plan. If your goal was to run a marathon, for example, and the farthest you'd ever run was a mile, twenty-six miles would feel pretty unattainable. In fact, it would be unattainable without a training program.

You would have to break the distance down into small, incremental steps that built one upon the other. In the first week, you'd push your mile to two. The next week, your goal would be three miles. And so on. Then by the time the race came around, you'd be ready.

Attainable translates to possible. For instance, if you're planning to write about a gunfight and feel it's essential to experience the kickback of the gun your character is going to use, you'd better be sure you can find that model and shoot it!

In Greta's *Mortician Murders* series, she decided early on she wouldn't go into a lot of detail about the embalming process. She wanted to do most of her research online without having to interview a mortician or visit a mortuary because of time constraints and the pandemic. It just wouldn't be possible to go on a field trip to a place dealing with an overabundance of possibly contagious bodies.

The good news was, the embalming process probably wasn't high on most mystery readers' wishlist. Sometimes less is more, and this was likely one of those times. These are the kinds of things to think about in this phase of goal setting.

Examples of Specific, Measurable, Attainable Writing Goals:

- Identify the top five most relevant research topics needed to flesh out my fictional world and how I plan to research them
- Based on the micro-goal I set in Chapter 12, add a target goal and a stretch goal to my daily or weekly word count.
- Decide if I'm going to revise my manuscript based on chapters or concepts and make a do-able revision list

Realistic and Time-Bound:

The next two steps of your SMART goal, realistic and time-bound, work together. As we've said before, it's difficult to know not only how long new things are going to take. However, it's also hard to know how those things are going to fit into our lives. Consequently, we set unrealistic goals, then feel like failures when we can't achieve them.

There are many books out there that promise if you follow their program, you'll write a novel in a month, or a short story every day, and it may be true. What the titles don't tell you, however, is that following their program isn't realistic for everyone.

For instance, we'd love to give you a hard and fast number of weeks for revising your novel. But frankly, that depends on how big of a mess it is when you start. For example, Greta's first published novel, *A Margin of Lust*, took her a year to revise on her own, then another three months with a professional editor. Six books later, she revised *The Peril of Pride* in two weeks on her own and another two with her editor.

Experience makes you faster at just about everything. So, take your experience level into consideration when figuring out how and where you're going to fit in the various tasks that you'll be tackling. It's better to err on the side of generosity.

We suggest taking the specific, measurable, attainable tasks you've listed in the above exercises, guesstimate how long they'll take and schedule them.

We go into more detail on how to do this in the next chapter, but in brief: if you have two hours a day on most weekdays to work on your book, and you've also decided you can write 1,000 words in two hours and that you're going to aim for a 70,000 word manuscript, you're looking at about 70 working days to completion.

Grab your calendar, cross out holidays, birthdays, days with doctor's appointments, weekends if you don't plan to work on them, etc. Give yourself a margin of a week or two for unforeseen circumstances. And you arrive at about four months for first drafting.

Examples of SMART Writing Goals:

- Identify the top five (or ten) most relevant research topics needed to flesh out my fictional world and how I plan to research them. Divide them into manageable daily chunks and plot them on my calendar.

- Decide how much time I have to write each day or each week, set a word count that seems attainable within that time frame, and plot it.
- Decide if I'm going to revise my manuscript based on chapters or concepts, make a revision list, then estimate a comfortable deadline based on my calendar.

Activity: Create at least three SMART goals for your current phase of writing.

Chapter 14
Finding the Time to Write

Everything we talked about in earlier chapters is based on mathematics and metrics. We're sure you're an intelligent person. You bought our book, after all. Intelligent people can grasp the phases of book creation, decide on their research and writing processes, and set SMART goals. In a perfect world, this book would be a short one. The first two sections would have set you up for success. Problem is, this isn't a perfect world.

Steven Pressfield has written a brilliant book called *The War of Art*. In it, he discusses a concept he calls Resistance, with a capital R. The idea is, whenever we decide to do something positive, something personally world changing, everything around us seems to conspire to hold us back.

Megan is a stay-at-home mom with two children under the age of ten. Her time is pretty limited. However, in the last eight years, she's written and published five full-length novels, a novella, a short story for an anthology, co-authored and published a non-fiction guidebook for writers, produced an accompanying course, and taught live workshops throughout Southern California and online. Whew.

How does she find the time and motivation to write when

she's exhausted from chasing kids, driving all over town, and managing a household?

The answer is two-fold. First, she prioritizes every activity in her life. Second, she uses every spare minute she can find.

Prioritization is key. It may seem obvious, but to do one thing, we must say no to another. As trite as it may sound, we have to let go of the good to fit the great into our lives. If we really want to be writers, we must prioritize it.

When Megan is in high production mode, she doesn't watch TV Sunday through Thursday nights. She's also given up video games—an old passion. When her girls are in school, she puts her butt in a chair and writes. She doesn't do laundry during that time (enormous sacrifice; we know) and sometimes the breakfast dishes sit in the sink until after dinner.

We joked above, but prioritizing writing over chores can actually be difficult. Parents with young children, in particular, often feel guilty for taking time away from the family. This is especially true in the early days, when writing isn't generating any income.

We suggest taking the time to think this through. Often, people unknowingly sabotage their writing goals because when it comes down to it they feel they're being irresponsible. However, if you wait to write until all the chores are done, the kids, your partner, and your dog are completely happy, chances are you'll never do it.

Speaking of partners, it's a good idea to run your goals by them. If your significant other is feeling ignored or resentful, this is a recipe for disaster as well. Creativity is hard enough without adding a bunch of family drama into the mix.

Our suggestion, now that you understand the breadth of the tasks and the time they'll take, is to give this writing thing a good hard think. Are you really willing to devote the time it will take? Perhaps, it would be better to postpone that novel until your baby hits second grade, or your spouse finishes their degree, or you've housebroken the puppy.

Okay, pep-talk over. If you're still reading, it's time to prioritize on paper.

One of the most important exercises we have students do in our productivity classes is to pull out a blank hourly planner and find the empty spaces in their typical week.

Here's Megan's example:

- First, she blocks off all the non-negotiable events: school drop-off and pickups, kids' after school lessons, sports, meetings (even the writing ones), etc.
- Once that's done, she schedules physical and mental health breaks: workouts, meditation sessions, yoga classes, couch time with her husband, even sleep.
- Finally, she looks at her planner and finds the blank spaces in her routine. This is her potential writing time.

Scheduling it makes it real. We use a brightly colored pen so that it grabs our attention. As much as possible, we don't let other life needs encroach on our writing time. It's sacred.

As mentioned in Chapter 12, writing every day at the same time helps to train our brains for creativity. However, that's not always possible, and for some people, it might even be counterproductive. Instead, find what works for you. If your schedule is crazy during the week, but you can dedicate Saturday and Sunday mornings for two hours, do that.

If you're looking at your schedule and not seeing much white space, don't despair. Any progress is forward progress, even if it's broken into five-minute chunks. Here are a few ideas to help you find those extra minutes in your day.

Suggestion One: Use Mobile Apps and Sync Across Devices

There are several great apps that can help you take your writing on the road. Scrivener (our choice for word processing) has mobile apps for iOS devices, including the iPhone and iPad. Evernote and Bear are both great tools for note-taking and short-form writing.

You can even use Google Docs on your devices, which gives you a free word processor with no hassle. Another advantage to Google Docs is its share-ability. If you're co-writing a book, like we're doing right now, it's easy for everyone involved to take part and it keeps each draft of the book fresh.

Once you have a way to get your writing off the desktop, you no longer need to have your butt in a chair to get your words on the page. We've written in doctors' waiting rooms, in cars, at kids' sporting events, and in coffee shops between errands.

Suggestion Two: Quit Facebook, Start Writing

Try implementing a social-media fast. Instead, use that time to create, not consume.

Stuck in line at Costco? Whip out your phone and write a few lines or outline a scene. Sitting through your daughter's Tae Kwon Do class? That's forty-five minutes of prime writing time. Stuck commuting on a train? You're golden. That's how Megan began writing fiction.

Suggestion Three: Wake Up Early

This is painful for many, but try it. You may find that the difficulty of waking up early is worth it if it improves your productivity. Sounds obvious, but the best way to make it happen is to go to bed a bit earlier at night. Also, painful for many. But really, how many Netflix series can we binge watch?

Megan gave this a whirl after reading *The Miracle Morning for Writers*. The reality is she's not a morning person, so it seemed a stretch. Her brain doesn't fully turn on until 8:00 after several cups of coffee. Her most productive hours are between 9:00 AM and noon.

However, she made the concept work for her with a few modifications. She realized she needed little brain power to exercise, start a load of laundry, or filter through emails. If she got chores out of the way early, then she could reserve her productive hours for guilt and distraction-free writing.

Greta uses this concept a little differently. She's found she is very creative first thing in the morning, but the day's chores loom over her, making this the hardest time to write. Instead of completing an hour-long sprint or trying to accomplish her entire word goal for the day, she's added a micro-goal into her morning routine—50 words. That's it.

She's found that completing 50 words (which often turns into 150) sets a creative tone. Her brain churns on the story throughout the day. When she has time to sit and get the bulk of the words on the page, she's faster and more efficient.

Suggestion Four: Get Creative To Be Creative

Sometimes it's necessary to frame situations in a different light to see opportunities we'd otherwise miss. For example, when Megan had a newborn, she wrote standing at the kitchen counter while bouncing her infant to sleep in a baby carrier. Not only did she get words on the page, but the baby got a solid nap *and* she got some exercise—multitasking at its finest.

A quick note on multitasking. We've all heard it is less productive, and we believe that's true. However, if you pair a brainless activity—like walking or riding an exercise bike or jiggling a baby—with writing, it's not a poor fit. Especially if you won't get anything done if you don't. Nothing is less productive than something.

But how do you write while walking, riding an exercise bike, or driving? The answer is dictation. If you're trying to accomplish an actual first draft, with all the punctuation included, there are software programs like Dragon that will pop out a rough version of your manuscript. You'll find yourself with a pretty hefty edit using this method, so if you plan to try it, take that into consideration when goal setting.

The downside of dictation is its steep learning curve. There are entire books on the topic. However, even if you can't use it for drafting, there are other uses. Recording notes, brainstorming, or outlining with dictation can speed up the process when you sit down to write.

When Greta was writing her third novel, she talked through an entire subplot by using voice typing in Gmail and sent it to herself. Once she had this very messy outline, she broke it into scenes, then copied and pasted each scene idea into its own document. The scene ideas worked as daily writing assignments.

Activity:

1. Work through the calendar exercise explained above. Block out unmissable events and essential

chores, then find the blank spaces and schedule some writing time.

2. Try out your favorite time-capturing suggestion from this chapter. Give yourself at least a week or two to see if it works for you.

Chapter 15
Structuring Your Schedule

I n Chapter 14, we discussed how the world seems to conspire against us once we decide to do something productive, and we gave you some things to do about it. But what about when you conspire against yourself?

When the pandemic hit, Greta began acquiring what's known in her household as "The COVID 15." This is the pudge that comes from wearing nothing other than leggings and PJs and deciding happy hour is now a nightly occurrence.

This was untenable. She actually did many things to fix the problem, but the one that relates to writing was that she downloaded the WW app on her phone. The app worked for her because it gave her wiggle room. On top of the daily allowable food points, there were 31 weekly bonus points. She hardly ever used them, but it was nice to know they were there in a pinch.

Greta's schedule during the pandemic was a bit like her overstuffed refrigerator. There were too many choices. It was a blank slate.

While many of you may have a time-shortage problem, Greta's was the exact opposite. She had so many hours of alone time, she procrastinated, got side-tracked, and wasted the time she had. She needed some hard edges on her schedule because, although she had a ton to do, she could do it pretty much any time she wanted.

Structure is a funny thing, though. Too little leads to procrastination, but too much can cause rebellion. Turning into her own drill sergeant didn't work any better than pampering herself. She'd tried scheduling her day within an inch of its life with every five minutes accounted for, potty breaks at three-hour intervals even if she was dancing around. Didn't work.

When planning her schedule last year, she had an Oprah moment. If wiggle room works for weight loss, why not for her writing life? (That's a whole lot of W's.)

She decided to try the wiggle-room method. Instead of no edges and no motivation, or drill-sergeant scheduling and rebelliousness, she scheduled her life in blocks. Each time block gave her plenty of time to do what needed to be done, and she used a timer to remind her when her time was up.

First she looked at the problem areas–the places she knew she was wasting time. Her morning starts with a devotional, prayer, and meditation. It's *spiritual,* right? Not so much. Half the time she was checking email and Facebook.

The solution: She made a rule for herself, no email or internet until she'd finished her morning routine, made the bed, and gotten dressed. She also set a timer for 7:00 as her end time. That hard edge pushed her to do what she was supposed to do instead of messing around.

Her second problem was that she got really into business projects while she was doing them, then lost track of time. She'd look up from her computer and hours and hours would have gone by, leaving her no time to work on her manuscript.

The solution: She slotted two hours every day for the business of writing. When that time was up, it was up. She moved the remaining tasks to the next day.

The third problem was actually getting words on the page. She realized she wrote quickly when she knew what she was supposed to write. She hemmed and hawed when she didn't have clarity.

The solution: This one was two-fold. First, she built plenty of plotting and research time into her schedule. She gave herself an entire week before she began a story, then slotted in a couple of days every three weeks in case she ran into a snag. In other words, wiggle room.

The second solution was the small habit mentioned in the previous chapter: writing 50 words as a part of her morning routine before finishing her coffee. This one tiny ritual got her brain cogitating on her story and made her writing time later in the day more effective. She'd been thinking about the story for hours, so she knew exactly what she needed to write.

The changes worked. She exceeded her goals most weeks and felt like she'd gained control. It wasn't perfect. She had to make adjustments, but that's the point. We can't expect perfection. Just progress.

If you see yourself procrastinating, wasting time, or rebelling, be creative. We've tried writing sprints with friends both online and in person, changing writing locations if home is too distracting, and writing with a timer. Even moving from one room to another when switching tasks can trigger your brain to change modes.

Activity:

1. Sit down and write out the ways you waste what could be productive time, then brainstorm some solutions.
2. Choose one of your solutions to implement today. Test it out for at least a week. If it works, great! If not, swap it out for something different. Keep experimenting until you find a habit that works for you.

Chapter 16
Writing More Efficiently

Time is money—you've heard that a few times, we're sure. Well, never is it more true than in the writing world. Each book, each short story, each magazine article you write is a product. The more products you have to sell, the more money you can make.

Of course, this isn't universally true. There are authors who hit it big with the first book and those who've written 50 that don't do well. However, for most, the more you write, the more you earn.

Productivity, as discussed in previous chapters, has many facets: self-discipline, avoiding distractions, setting aside a certain time slot, and on and on. One thing we haven't touched on yet, however, is flow.

Flow is that state where all distractions fade into the background, your story comes to life in your mind, and it seems you're simply recording what you're seeing. When you're in the flow, words fly from your fingers, and they're actually good words. You laugh and cry with your characters.

Many of us have been there, and when we are, we often find we write much faster. Sometimes three or four times faster than our normal pace. It's kind of magical.

The obvious question is: can you control flow? Yes, and no. Chris Fox teaches a course based on his book 5,000 Words Per Hour: Write Better Faster. The first thing he teaches about is setting up your zone, or your space. He says you can achieve flow through brain training.

When Greta was a runner, she had a set of rituals she performed before every race. She ate toast with peanut butter and honey an hour or more before the event. She tied her shoelaces a certain way. When she arrived at the track, she performed a particular set of warm-up exercises.

She believed she was doing these things for her body, that peanut butter and just-right shoelaces and warm-up exercises would give her an advantage. There was truth in that, but it was also true that she was mentally preparing herself for flow. She was signaling her brain to take her into a runner's high. Sometimes it worked. Sometimes it didn't.

So, how can you set yourself up for flow? What's the writer's equivalent of shoelace knots? Mihaly Csikszentmihalyi, a Croatian psychologist, is best known for his study of the flow state. His book, *Flow: The Psychology of Optimal Experience*[1], popularized the concept. In brief, these are the things Csikszentmihalyi recommends for achieving this high productivity state.

Begin With a Level of Mastery

If you're just starting out, it will be difficult or impossible to reach a flow state. If you're still learning basic chords on the guitar, you won't be able to reach flow while performing a piece of music. It may not take Malcolm Gladwell's 10,000 hours, but we need a certain level of mastery in a craft to achieve flow. If you're not there yet, keep on practicing.

Have a Clear Goal

Even if you're a "pantser" or "discovery writer" who doesn't like to outline, you'll need defined parameters for the writing session. Are you going to write a 1,000 word scene? Where does it take place? Who's in it? What is the purpose of the scene? Knowing these things before you write will help you get into the flow faster. Therefore, we suggest scheduling as much time as you need for research and plotting. Ultimately, the time will be regained in writing speed.

Create as Distraction-Free an Environment as Possible

As Chris Fox talks about in his course, setting up a place and a time can lead to a successful writing session. Not only are you eliminating distractions—turning off the internet, getting comfortable, having your water or coffee or whiskey at your elbow—but these things can be the signals we discussed earlier. Some people light scented candles, some put on certain types of music, some eat peanut butter and honey toast. Find what works for you.

Refuse to Edit Yourself or Worry About Failure

This is the hardest part of the process for Greta. She's tried many tricks, but gamifying the process works best for her. We cover this in the section on Pomodoros.

Enjoy the Activity for its Own Sake

Again, sometimes easier said than done. Since we've been

published, we often look at writing as "work" instead of play. We had a lot more fun with our stories before we had contracts, editors, and reviewers. So, if you're just starting out, enjoy the freedom.

If you're in the same boat we are, try reminding yourself that no one is going to read what you've written in its current state. You'll be editing before any other eyes are on the work.

Tools to Help You Enter the Flow State

Csikszentmihalyi's suggestions can work for anyone in any field, but how about some writing specific tools to assist you to get in the flow? Our two favorites are braindumps and Pomodoros.

While Megan's greatest challenge is finding the time to write, Greta's is mindset. If she's not in the right frame of mind, the entire writing process morphs from creative dance to chain-gang shuffle. Insecurity is the ball and chain. The two things that breed that insecurity are not knowing what she should write, and doubting her ability to write it even if she does.

Psychologists estimate the average person in a first world country makes somewhere around 35,000 decisions a day. Apparently, we use two separate methods. One is the logical examination of options. The second is more unconscious and emotionally driven—the gut reaction.

Obviously, the first is more time-consuming and tiring. We have limited resources for logical decision making. After 50 to seventy-five of them, we run out of steam. The gut reaction process is both quicker and much less exhausting for our brains.

Plotters have an easier time with this problem than pantsers because they make many decisions in advance. However, even when we know the general story, there are plenty of gritty details we must hash out on the page. And there's something incredibly intimidating about a blank screen and a blinking cursor. It's the equivalent of a computer impatiently tapping its fingers.

Therefore, if we can reduce the number of logic driven decisions we have to make when we sit down to write, we will write faster and without as much stress. Hence the braindump.

Here's How Braindumps Work:

You open a fresh clean document, check your Fiction Plot Map, outline, or whatever you've used to plan your day-to-day work and discover you need to write chapter five.

What do you know about chapter five already? Can you answer these questions in brief?

- Where does the scene take place?
- Who is in it?
- What's the point?
- Where's the tension?

Once you've answered these questions, it's time to dump. You can set a timer for this exercise, or you can just write until you're done. Your choice. We rarely time a dump.

Close your eyes if you can type with your eyes shut and visualize the scene you plan to write as if it were a movie. Now take snapshots with your words. What are you seeing, sensing, hearing, and feeling? Don't write in full sentences. Separate the words and phrases by commas only. Don't worry about grammar, spelling, word choice, or anything writerly. Go!

Here is a brief example from *To Dye For*, a book Greta will release early 2022:

Imogene enters, cold, sterile, white tiles, floor is concave, a drain at the center, smells of chemicals, gurney near drain, woman in green dress lying on it, it's Trudy, loss, repulsion, comes closer, peaceful, Carlton too cheerful, makeup, hair dye, all in bag, he turns to leave, fear, don't leave me, he says Trudy won't bite

Can you see how many decisions she made in these few lines? Not only that, but by visualizing instead of trying to logic it out, she pushed her brain into instinct mode. Now when she actually writes the scene, the only decisions she has to make are about word choice, phrasing, and so on. She already knows the setting, the mood, and what happens.

Try Gamifying Your Writing with Pomodoros

Once you've got your brain dump at the top of your page, it's time to write the scene. To harken back to the ball and chain analogy, if not knowing what to write is the ball, doubting your skill is the chain. The best way we've found to stop doubting our skill is to stop thinking about it.

Here's an experiment: Don't think about an elephant.

Of course, everyone has just imagined the big, gray beast. The only way to stop thinking about an elephant is to think about a rabbit—or something else. Enter the Pomodoro.

A Pomodoro is a fancy way of saying a work sprint. They've been used in business settings for years, but they can be especially helpful for flow-state activities.

All you have to do is set your timer for 25 minutes and start writing. Don't let yourself edit or delete anything, instead focus on getting as many words on the page as possible. When the timer goes off, take a five minute break, record the number of words you wrote, then repeat the process. We like to see if we can improve on our previous word counts with each writing sprint.

Pomodoros force your brain to think about something else, like numbers. Instead of wringing your hands over the keyboard, you're sprinting, seeing how fast your fingers can fly. By turning it into a game, you're giving yourself a serotonin hit with every sprint. You never know... just one more sprint and you might break your personal record.

But what if they're terrible words?

That's not the concern at the moment. The concern is quantity, not quality. Besides, according to Malcolm Gladwell's book *Blink*, intuitive decisions are often better than conscious ones. And, remember, you can't edit a blank page. Fixing the bloopers comes in the revision stage of writing.

Measure to Manage

Whether you use Pomodoros to boost your writing speed or not, we recommend creating a writing diary to track your progress. After all, if you don't know where you are, how can you get where you want to go? If you don't know how fast you write, how do you know when your manuscript will be done, then how can you manage your production schedule?

Unfortunately, humans are fickle beasts and sometimes we don't actually *want* to know where we are. We're afraid of what those measurements might reveal. What if it proves we can't meet our goals? Worse, what if it turns out we're slower than every other writer on the planet? (We guarantee that's not true).

Or perhaps we fear changing because we're comfortable where we are. It's easier to put on the blinders and keep plodding along than it is to challenge ourselves to make improvements. Change is hard. Change is scary.

We get it. We love a schedule and solid routine. Ask either of us about our latest planner, and you'll see what we mean. But without change, we stagnate. Without challenges, our writing grows stale. If we want to be professional writers, we must strive to improve both in craft and in execution.

If you've read and implemented the previous chapters, you have your schedule mapped out and are building a productive writing habit. Now it's time to shine a spotlight on your accomplishments. Remember, every word is one step closer to a completed manuscript.

There are several ways to track your writing. The easiest is to write your daily word count (or chapters edited, or research done) next to the goal you've already projected on your calendar.

Greta puts "MW" and "DW" on each working day of her planner. When she completes her morning words, she writes the number next to the MW. When she completes the day's words, she writes it next to the DW. At the end of the week, she writes her total words for the week and the total word count of her manuscript to see if she's on track. If she isn't, she can troubleshoot.

Megan really loves spreadsheets and data, so she's more creative with her diary. She built an Excel spreadsheet to track each writing sprint, the day and time, the word count for that sprint and the resulting words per hour, qualitative data that may have influenced her session (e.g. music, mood, interruptions, etc.) She then uses that information to optimize her writing time. It has helped her go from a few hundred words per hour to over a thousand. For a discovery writer, that's pretty fast.

If this sounds daunting, never fear. You can access a free

version of Megan's spreadsheet when you join The Author Wheel community at www.AuthorWheel.com/Foundations. If it still sounds daunting, you can use Greta's method. The method isn't as important as the doing.

Activity:

1. Set up a writing diary either in an existing calendar or use a spreadsheet. Record how many words you're writing each day.
2. Try doing a brain dump before your next three writing sessions. Assess how you felt after each session. Did you achieve a flow state? Did you get more words on the page?
3. Try using the Pomodoro technique to gamify your writing. Can you beat your previous word count?

Chapter 17
Avoiding Burnout

One often repeated bit of writerly advice is: Get your butt in the chair. While it's true, you must be in front of a computer to write, what you do with the rest of your day may mean the difference between a writing career and a single book. Inactivity, screen time, and seclusion come with a price tag. Let's tackle the sedentary problem first.

Greta used to work in a gym, now she writes. She found the transition extremely difficult. She exercises every day and thought that would solve the problem. However, one hour of exercise in the morning isn't enough to combat the ill effects of sitting for hours on end. Research says sitting is the new smoking. It's killing America and much of the developed world.

Here are some things that happen when you sit for long periods of time:

- Decreased ability to metabolize fats
- Increased risk of heart disease, certain cancers, diabetes, metabolic syndrome, and obesity
- Increased incidence of anxiety and depression

Need proof? According to a New York Times Magazine

article titled "Is Sitting a Lethal Activity,"[1] Dr. Marc Hamilton (Pennington Biomedical Research Center) recruited 14 young, thin people and tracked the results of inactivity on their bodies. In only 24 hours, he recorded a 40% reduction in their insulin's ability to uptake glucose. They were already showing symptoms of pre-diabetes.

So what's a writer to do? This is a dilemma. In order to write, we need to sit. In order to be healthy, we can't. Add to that the fact that many writers fall prey to carpal tunnel, neck and spinal issues, and low back pain. Sorry Stephen King (or whoever coined the "butt in chair" phrase) the body wasn't designed for inactivity.

The good news is, we don't have to give up writing and become construction workers or marathon runners. We just need to move more. Dr. James Levine from the Mayo Clinic did an interesting study with magic underwear.[2] We can't buy it, but we can learn from it.

His subjects wore special, neoprene clothing that tracked every slight muscle movement they made. They didn't exercise and ate carefully monitored meals. When Dr. Levine increased the calories of the individuals, he learned something interesting about who gained weight and who didn't.

He called his findings N.E.A.T.–Non-Exercise Activity Thermogenesis. In layperson's language, he found the people who didn't gain weight, despite the calorie increase, burned it up through movement. They sat less. They walked around, fidgeted, did chores, and ran up and down stairs more. Even easy walking or pacing burns an extra 130 calories an hour.

Here are a few ways we can apply that principal to our writing lives:

- Do Pomodoros, as we mentioned above, and move on your five-minute breaks. Greta often combines exercise with writing. She rides a stationary bike for 30 minutes before she starts work, then uses her suspension trainer, or lifts weights, or does Yoga during the five-minute intervals.
- Try dictating while you walk. As mentioned in Chapter 2, dictating is not only a time saver, but it can be a lifesaver as well. There are lots of free and paid programs that will transcribe your words. Neither of us has mastered dictation for actual content, but we've found it helpful for brainstorming sessions.
- Sit on a stability ball instead of a chair and rotate your hips while you write.
- Schedule your in-person meetings out on a trail if possible.
- Take your phone calls on the road. If you can't leave the house, get up and pace.
- Use a standup desk. When you step back to read or ponder your work, step side to side.

Another health problem associated with writing and many other careers is that too much screen time can lead to depression and sleeplessness. If we write all morning, scroll through social media in the afternoon, and watch TV at night to unwind, we're headed for trouble.

Greta's cousin gave her a birthday card that says: *Life is what happens when you're not looking at a screen.* She pinned it to her bulletin board. We don't know about you, but we need to get away from our virtual friends and spend time with our real ones every day for mental health.

Hobbies are terrific for your emotional state as well, especially active ones. Greta kayaks, is learning to cook vegan meals, and does knitting and crocheting projects in front of the TV to help keep her eyes off the screen. Megan lifts weights, plays piano, and walks her girls to and from school every day to absorb some much needed sunshine and fresh air.

You may also find that without a regular recharge, your creative well runs dry. The more activities we can do that *aren't* writing, the more inspiration we'll have to pull from.

Traveling is a great example. Travel helps us incorporate cultural and architectural influences into our work. By noting our surroundings and our sensory experiences, our descriptions and settings will feel more real. Google Earth is great for research, but it can't replace experience.

Finally, too much solitude can lead to depression and burnout. Even introverts need to get out sometimes.

Many writers will tell you they are introverts. Megan is one of them. Sometimes people are surprised by that because she's not shy or socially awkward. Although she does better in small gatherings than at large parties, she can almost always find a friendly conversation and enjoy herself when she has to attend the latter. She teaches courses and workshops with as many as 50 people in a class. And in a previous life, she gave presentations in front of hundreds of people. Introvert obviously doesn't mean wallflower.

So how do we define "introvert?" It's a complicated topic. Books have been written about it, but for our purposes, introverts are individuals who find large social occasions tiring, but solitude calming and revitalizing. They often need to be alone to recalibrate and recharge. Sounds like most writers we know, doesn't it?

When the pandemic hit in 2020, Megan thought she would have no problem with quarantining, lockdowns, or the restrictions against gatherings. She actually looked forward to the alone time. Finally, an excuse to hoard her energy, wear sweats all day, and avoid small talk. Perhaps many of you felt the same.

But at the writing of this book, we are entering our third year of Covid and many of us are coming to realize the importance of breaking out of our shells. It's fine to spend an evening at home, but isolation can atrophy our social skills, limit our writing and creative energy, and lead to depression. It's a recipe for burnout.

Networking is more important than we think. Meeting new people means synergism. The more connections we make, the more opportunities come our way. In the past, we might have achieved this by attending writers' conferences or critique groups. Nowadays, it's more difficult.

However, even non-writing-related networking has its benefits—after all, you never know when you might meet someone whose sister is also a writer (this was how Megan got her first critique partner), or whose brother is an illustrator and a pro at book covers.

Networking makes it easier to find reputable contractors (like editors and cover designers) which takes some of the guesswork out of the writing and publishing process. A positive network can answer questions, help us clarify our goals, and show us what's possible in our craft and career.

And when we meet writers, we often find they make great friends.

When we first started writing, we didn't have any writer friends. In fact, both of us were hesitant to tell anyone other than our husbands that we were trying to write novels. It wasn't until we went to our first writers' conference that we even *felt* like we could call ourselves writers.

Conferences are a great place to find comrades in arms. We met at a conference many years ago and have been a support for each other ever since. Everyone is there for the same reason: to talk and to learn about writing craft and the publishing industry. It's such a refreshing change from sitting at our computers alone, struggling to understand what we are doing and why. It's where we find our tribe, people who just *get it*–who get us.

Writers' groups are another place to connect with our tribe. We each belong to several. Each one has its own focus and purpose, but all of them give us an outlet to share our joys and frustrations. Writers speak the same language about the publishing industry and laugh at the same inside jokes. Without them, the only people we could talk to about our stories would be our husbands—who *aren't* fiction authors. Our writer friends have probably saved our sanity and our marriages.

You can't brainstorm without a team. One of the best outcomes of regular get-togethers with other writers is idea brainstorming. Critique partners bounce plot problems off each other and break through writers' block. Genre-based writers' groups discuss trends in the industry or tropes that are popular in the kinds of books they write. Marketing groups share tools and tactics that make it easier to find new readers and build an audience.

The more you share your writing life, the more you talk through your challenges and hash out your ideas, the stronger your stories and your business will be. Plus, you might find yourself inspired to try something new or do something you would never have thought of on your own.

Which brings us to the last benefit of getting out there, or letting others in: motivation. When we sit by ourselves in our isolated writing caves, it can feel like we're stuck in the dark, struggling to find the light switch to illuminate our work. Too much solitude can make us feel like failures, even when we're making good progress. We can become so overwhelmed by the book or the business it seems impossible to finish or to find an audience if we do.

When we open the door to writer friends, the illumination we need naturally shines in. We have someone to keep us accountable and to cheer us on. Outside eyes often recognize the progress and the skill that we don't see in ourselves.

Allowing the success of others to inspire instead of intimidate challenges us to think bigger, do more, and tackle things in new ways. Breaking out of solitude might make the difference between forward progress and stagnation.

Activity:

1. Write three ways you can incorporate a little more movement into your everyday activities. Post the list near your work area to remind you to move.
2. Consider your non-writing activities: What hobbies do you enjoy now? What activities would you like to pursue? Pursue a couple.
3. Research writing groups. Facebook is a great place to start online, or Google in-person meet-ups in your local area. Challenge yourself to take part in at least one new community this week.

Part Four

Designing Your Author Career Strategy

Chapter 18
What is Strategy and Why is it Important?

Publishing is complicated. There are myriad ways to be successful, and what works for one person might not work for another.

Some writers can produce six books a year (or more!) and not break a sweat. Others have day jobs they love and can only put out one book a year. Some authors are pushing for a six-figure full-time income from their writing. Others write for the joy of storytelling and aren't as concerned about the money.

Those with digital design, marketing, or data analysis backgrounds have helpful business skills. Those without those skills will have to take courses, find publishers, or hire help. We are unique. Each writer must walk their own path to publication based on their goals, skills, and definitions of success.

That's where strategy comes in.

An author strategy is a living document that maps your unique path to a sustainable career. It is a guide that will help you clarify your purpose, simplify your process, and implement tactics that will keep you moving toward success as *you* define it.

We've said it before; you have to know where you are in order to know where you're going. When it comes to author strategy, we take it one step further. You not only need to know where you are but also who you are and what you want in order to blaze a path to your best future.

In this section, we'll discuss three processes: clarification, simplification, and implementation.

Clarification asks why you're doing what you're doing. It helps you define your purpose and communicate that purpose to your audience. We'll go into clarity in more detail in Chapters 19 and 20 as you craft your author mission statement and personal tagline.

However, the publishing business is a tangled web of possibilities these days. Simplification helps us to choose which threads to pull and which to leave alone. We'll tackle simplification in Chapters 21 and 22 as you learn to lean into your strengths and overcome your weaknesses.

Finally, in Chapters 23 and 24, you'll set goals, create an actual plan with action steps, and begin to implement those steps.

As you develop your author strategy, remember that this is a living document. It's not something you complete once and forget about. It will grow and change as you do. With each revolution of the author wheel, you'll learn more about your books and yourself, develop new skills, and pursue new goals. But as long as you continue to clarify, simplify, and implement, you'll stay on the road to your dreams.

Action Plan:

1. Find a blank notebook or open a word doc dedicated to your author strategy. In the next

chapters, you'll be journaling and brainstorming. It will be helpful to keep it all in one place!

2. On the first page of your new journal, we want you to dream big. Spend five to ten minutes freewriting: What is your Big Dream? Do you want to be a six-figure author? Will your publisher book you on a national book tour, where you'll sign books at stores across the country? Will you have a movie deal? Give yourself free rein to make your dream as big and crazy as you can. No one will read this but you. We'll come back to the Big Dream in Chapter 23, so be prepared.

3. Next, write your personal purpose for creating an author career strategy. What are you hoping to gain from this process?

Chapter 19
Self-Discovery

I f you were starting a business, you'd probably write a mission statement. It's Business 101. Banks and investors won't back a confusing, ill-conceived project.

Guess what? If you're an author, you're a businessperson. You're creating a product that you want other people to buy.

As an indie author, that business may seem obvious. You must write the book, and hire a cover designer, create a marketing plan, and decide which platforms you want to sell on and the price of each book.

Traditionally published authors often *think* they don't need to be business minded, but they're wrong. Their publisher will handle many—but not all—of the product packaging, marketing, and sales decisions. However, the author signs the contract that allows them to do it. Those terms will determine if they get to decide what their next project will be and how they reach readers. These days, the author is usually as much a part of the branding as the book.

Understanding yourself and your goals will help you take control of your future. After all, if we don't fully understand our purpose, how can we tell others what it is? And if we can't tell others, how can we find our audience and market our books?

Most fiction authors would say their mission is to make money or write a certain number of books a year or get an agent and a traditional deal. While all these goals are great, they aren't a mission statement. They are pieces of a strategy.

A mission statement, in its most simplistic form, is a declaration of motive. For writers, it answers the question: Why do you write what you write?

The goal of this chapter is to give you some things to think about to help you arrive at an answer.

If you're worried this will be time consuming or complicated...don't be. Mission statements don't have to be ten page documents. If you aren't asking for a loan, they can be brief. For instance, the abbreviated Author Wheel mission statement is to help writers overcome their roadblocks through books, courses, and a podcast so they can keep their stories rolling.

To arrive at that, we had to do some soul searching. We knew we wanted to create a business that helped writers, but how? What made our message unique? How did we plan to deliver it? Answering those questions enabled us to create a blueprint and a tagline for business growth.

When it comes to nonfiction, particularly educational or self-help material, you could argue that mission statements are a little easier to pin down. The audience is obvious. An understanding of their needs is probably what drew you to the subject to begin with.

Creatives, on the other hand, often skip this step, even when we hope to pay the bills with our royalties. Often, we make whatever we think our muse is leading us to make, then cross our fingers and hope it finds an audience. While this might be fulfilling on one level, it can also be pretty demoralizing if we don't get that lightning strike we were praying for.

In our defense, it's more difficult for us as fiction writers to figure out the business side of our careers. We may not have a clear picture of who the audience for our stories is or why they'd choose our books over some seven-figure author's. Our product is ourselves, and we're complex creatures. However, it's just as important for creatives to understand what they're attempting as it is for a plumber, a dentist, or a lawyer to understand their specialty and purpose.

The first step in developing your author strategy is one of self-discovery, so now's the time to grab your journal.

As you read the following questions and explanations, we suggest you write your thoughts as you go. Keep your journal close and jot down whatever comes to mind as it arises. The more time and space you give yourself to examine your early influences and personal interests, the easier it will be to craft your mission statement.

Since we're readers first, let's start with story.

Mission Statement Part 1: What are your favorite genres to read? Who were your earliest literary influences?

Stories help us process life. They teach us how to navigate difficulties and challenges. Through them, we're able to experience things vicariously that we might never experience in real life. They're powerful.

Not every story appeals to every person. In fact, the fiction we're most attracted to tells us a lot about our fears and motivations.

For instance, many psychologists believe that those who love mysteries and thrillers view people as their greatest threat. Readers want to face their fears from the safety of their armchairs and learn how to defeat the villains by watching others do it. They're seeking societal and personal safety and have a strong desire to see justice done.

Romance readers are looking for a human connection. Their greatest fears may revolve around loneliness or rejection. Through story, they can explore their own emotional highs and lows while finding comfort in the happily ever after.

Science Fiction readers are seeking the answers to the problems of humanity on a more global scale. They may fear political, technological, or even spiritual glitches. They want to believe they could survive a zombie apocalypse or colonize another planet.

We're often attracted to different forms of fiction at different stages of our lives. Greta loved *The Walking Dead* when she was between careers and wishing for a level playing field. That world was terrible, but everyone was in it together, relying on their brains and physical abilities to survive. When COVID came along, suddenly, the idea of a global pandemic hit too close to home. A zombie plague no longer provided an escape.

Unattached people or people in unhappy relationships might want more romance in their stories. Those deciding on a career path or entering a shaky job market might be drawn to stories that touch on politics or technology. And so on.

Of course, we're complex beings. That's why Rocky Road, Neapolitan, and Cherry Garcia ice creams were created. We like many things. From a literary perspective, this is how genre mashups happen.

For example:

- Romantic suspense—Thrillers with strong romantic elements or romances with strong thriller elements. These books appeal to readers who want to see the bad guy caught while indulging in a romantic happily ever after.

- Urban fantasy—Thriller or horror and fantasy. Readers of these stories are often looking for an exciting or gritty action adventure with otherworldly influences.
- Buddy romance—Adventure stories that focus on friendship rather than romance. However, they're still relationship driven.
- Dystopian fiction—Science fiction and horror come together in movies like *Alien* and books like *Hunger Games.*

Refer to the section on Understanding Your Genre if you need a refresher on what genre is and why it's important.

Most authors—or rather, pen names—specialize in one or two broad genres. Stephen King writes Horror. J. K. Rowling writes Young Adult Fantasy. Nora Roberts writes romance. These authors have all written under other pen names to clarify their readers' expectations.

Action Plan:

1. Think through what genres you've been the most drawn to throughout your life. What do you love to read?
2. Who are your favorite authors? Can you pinpoint why you love their stories? What is it about their writing that has you hooked?

Mission Statement Part 2: What types of characters, settings, and tropes attract you?

As we've said, most of us read and write to escape into an alternate reality. We want to have adventures we wouldn't normally have, sort through niggling issues and hang around with people who interest us.

For instance, Greta loves old houses near oceans or lakes, cabins in the woods, and journeys on planes, trains, or even spaceships. She can't resist stories in which the main character inherits a big house that needs to be remodeled, particularly if it's a haunted house. She loves mystery/thriller but, she'd be tempted by a fantasy novel set in a creepy old mansion near the ocean.

Megan loves fighting monsters and questing alongside heroes who strive to make the world a better place and find hope in the darkness. If there's a portal to another world, real or metaphorical, all the better.

Fantasy is her genre, but romance stories involving other cultures or "worlds" will tempt her when she's in the mood for a happily ever after.

Characters, settings, and tropes can pull us into genres we don't normally read, and they can shove us out of our favorite type of story as well. Most of us have started a book that seemed perfect—great setting, twisty tropes, right genre—only to stop reading because we couldn't find one character to relate to. Or, maybe, the characters were great, but it had a prison setting, and prison settings are a turnoff.

Action Plan:

1. In your journal, write a list of at least 5-10 tropes that you love. These could be objects, storylines, settings, or character types.
2. Which of these tropes occur in the stories that you've already written or plan to write?

Mission Statement Part 3: What impact do you want your stories to have?

A common mistake new writers make is to forget about the reader. They assume because they love their book, it will have universal appeal. Unfortunately, the book that *everybody* loves has never been written. Even the classics have negative reviews.

Perhaps you've never actually thought about the impact you want your books to make on readers, or you've only thought about it in vague terms. You want them to love it. You want it to be a page-turner. You want them to be fully immersed in the story.

These goals are great, but they aren't specific. They can apply to almost any book. Narrowing down the primary and secondary purposes of the stories you write can actually help you write your author mission statement.

There are three main story drivers:

- **Entertainment -** These stories usually have larger-than-life characters, fast moving plots, and significant settings. Think Clive Cussler, Janet Evanovich, and Marvel movies.

- **Education -** These stories often have unusual or quirky characters and strong societal or scientific themes. They're typically set in historical, cultural, or futuristic settings. Examples would be Linda Castillo's Amish Murder Mysteries, Michael Crichton's books and movies, and Kate Quinn's historical fiction.

- **Inspiration -** These stories often have relatable characters who are thrown into dire circumstances. The settings feel familiar even when they're fantastical. Great examples are C. S. Lewis's Chronicles of Narnia, John Grisham's stories, and the TV show *The Walking Dead*.

There are usually elements of all three drivers in our books, but one will rise above the others. And it may change from story to story. Greta's *Seven Deadly Sins Murders* series is primarily inspirational. Her *Mortician Murders* series is more entertainment driven. However, both are entertaining and inspirational because that's what she enjoys most in the stories she reads.

Megan's books are primarily entertainment, but they also have a strong educational element. She enjoys learning about the belief systems of other cultures and weaves their myths into her stories.

Based on the above definitions, what's the primary impact you hope your books will make on readers? What's the secondary impact? Think about descriptive adjectives that might convey that experience to readers.

Action Plan:

1. Spend some time thinking, meditating, or mulling on the three story drivers. Prioritize them in order of importance for your stories. If you have more than one series, consider whether the priorities are different for each series.

2. Make a list of descriptive adjectives that apply to your stories. Highlight your primary and secondary story drivers with creative words. Try to find words that have double meanings relevant to your books.

Mission Statement Part 4: What themes resonate with you the most?

Now it's time to look at the bigger picture. You've examined what draws you regarding story elements. However, there is something that ties all these elements together into one neat package, and that's *theme*.

Theme is the overriding message of a story. For instance, the theme of *To Kill a Mockingbird* is heroism. Atticus stands up against social injustice regardless of the impact it will make on him or his career. If you read that book or watch the movie with a careful eye, you'll notice all the primary characters face a version of that same dilemma.

Note, theme can be boiled down to a single word. As mentioned, in *To Kill a Mockingbird*, it's "heroism." In other stories, the theme might be "identity" or "justice" or "sacrifice." The theme is a single word that carries a lot of weight. It describes social, moral, ethical, and emotional dilemmas. It can often be identified by analyzing the internal conflicts of the characters.

The themes that resonate with you as a human being are most often the themes you choose to write about, either consciously or unconsciously. They are also the themes you find most satisfying when you consume fiction.

The themes you choose and how they relate to your chosen genre can make your writing unique. Although some themes fit more neatly into certain genres, exploring a common theme in uncommon ways can be exciting for readers.

For instance, a common theme in the mystery/thriller genre is justice. It's less common in romance. A romance novel that included all the typical romance beats but had a justice theme could be an interesting and unique story.

Theme tells a reader a lot about you, the author. Your take on the world will influence plot, character, and all the pieces of your fiction. Writers write to entertain, educate, and inspire, but they also write to work out the problems that keep them up at night.

If you're unsure what themes you're drawn to, think about your favorite books and movies. Do they have common themes? Have you stopped to figure out the themes of your own books?

Action Plan:

1. Think back to your early influences from Mission Statement Step 1. Can you identify any recurring themes in those books? Make a list of as many relevant single-word themes as possible.
2. Do the same thing for your own stories. What words define the conflict (internal or external) for your characters? What social or moral dilemmas do your characters face?
3. Compare what has influenced you to your own writing. Which themes are common to both lists?

Chapter 20
The Mission Statement & Tagline

Now it's time to use the answers to the questions posed in the last chapter to rough out a mission statement. Start by filling in the blanks.

I write (impact, genre) set in (setting). My protagonists are (types of characters) who (your favorite tropes) and/to/for (theme).

As an example, here's Megan's mission statement:

> I write action-packed (*entertainment*) portal fantasy adventures (*genre*) that cross between Earth and other realms (*setting*). My protagonists are strong women (*types*) who must face down the monsters that haunt them (*tropes*) to understand themselves and their place in the world. (*Belonging and Purpose are themes in my books*).

And here's Greta's mission statement:

> I write thoughtful and sometimes humorous (*inspirational and entertaining*) murder mysteries (*genre*) set in Southern

California (*setting*). My protagonists are flawed but courageous women (*types*) in life and death and sometimes otherworldly circumstances (*tropes*), who must face hard truths to save themselves and find justice for those they care about. (*Truth, Justice, and Belonging are all common themes in my books.*)

Experiment with different versions of your mission statement. Plug in different words from your theme list or impact list. Use a thesaurus to find even more. It may take several iterations before you're completely happy with it.

It's often helpful to share a few versions of your author mission statement with other writers who are familiar with your work, or readers who love your writing. They can help you find alternative words or phrases that might further clarify your purpose. We're rarely good at diagnosing ourselves, so discussing your mission with people who know you and your work well can be eye opening.

Once you work out your fill-in-the-blank statement, you can do several things with it. The first benefit is to use your mission statement as a guide for your future decisions.

Avoid Shiny-Thing Syndrome

Say you write portal fantasy adventures like Megan. You've been working hard to build your backlist and a base of fans who love what you write. Then one day you read that billionaire romances are selling by the truckload. You want to sell truckloads of books. Ergo, you decide to write a billionaire romance.

Unless you can figure out how these books jibe with your fantasy world, it's probably not a good idea. If you're dead set on it, you'll most likely need to create an entirely new pen name and online persona.

That's a lot of work, but the bigger problem is you. Do you like billionaire romances? Do they resonate with you? Do the tropes you love ever occur in these kinds of stories? Will your recurring theme of purpose or belonging work?

If you answer yes to those questions, you might take a percentage of your readership with you into your new venture. After all, people buy your first book because of genre and tropes. They buy the second, third and so on because of you, the author. If you love something, chances are at least some of them will too.

However, if you don't enjoy billionaire romances, and if the issues that tug at your heart and mind won't work as themes in these stories, don't write one. You'll sabotage your author brand, and the new books probably won't succeed, anyway.

There are authors who write in several genres and do well in all of them. However, if you read those stories, you'll often find they have more in common than you'd imagine. Although J. K. Rowling's Harry Potter series and her adult Cormoran Strike mysteries are meant for completely different audiences, there are a surprising number of commonalities between them.

Harry's parents didn't raise him, but their legacy influences his life. Cormoran's absentee father was a famous rockstar, something that will always affect him. Harry has a significant scar that symbolizes his destiny. Comoran has a prosthetic leg which symbolizes his destiny. Both characters have special abilities and are responsible for using them for the greater good of humanity. And we could go on.

The point is, those who grew up loving the Harry Potter series may be primed for a more adult version in Cormoran Strike. However, whether or not Harry fans crossover, Rowling has remained true to herself.

There are ways of crossing genre lines without ruffling too many feathers. Greta loves science fiction, but recognizes she can't write it without creating a new pen name. However, she can weave some science-fiction elements into her *Mortician Murders* series. In that way, she can scratch that itch while remaining true to her branding. Readers who love the way her (sometimes demented) mind works go along for the ride. Some of them like her better for it. Some of them wish she'd stick to more traditional mystery tropes, but there hasn't been a mass exodus.

Megan stepped off the fantasy adventure train to write an epic fantasy just before COVID. It wasn't a huge success.

The book is every bit as good as her other series, but it suffered from a few key problems. In part, it was timing. She tried to launch the book just as the world was going into lockdown. Her readers were a little preoccupied. Worse, Megan failed to meet her reader expectations.

Although the epic fantasy series was technically a prequel to *The Sanyare Chronicles* and many of the characters carried over between series, the tone and style were completely different. *The Sanyare Chronicles* is fast-paced and has a single point of view. *The War of the Nine Faerie Realms* is an epic with multiple point of view characters and broad political stakes. The scope of *The Sanyare Chronicles* is limited to the journey of a single character. *The War of the Nine Faerie Realms* details the court intrigue and competing agendas of no less than four different factions.

Those differences were enough to limit the crossover between the series. Most of her readers wanted more of *The Sanyare Chronicles*. They weren't interested in a big political drama, even if it was set in the same world. It just didn't work as well as Megan had hoped. Had she clarified her purpose and written her mission statement before writing the epic, she might have better understood what her readers were looking for from her writing and crafted the story differently.

Expand the mission statement into an ABOUT PAGE.

Fleshing out your mission statement is a great way to tell your readers what they can expect from your books. Instead of a boring bio, you can share a bit of your personality and purpose with your readers.

Keep in mind, however, that your audience isn't looking for a corporate slogan. Our little formula won't be persuasive to a potential reader. It will need to be polished and presented in a more entertaining way.

For example, Greta's ABOUT PAGE has two sections: *Things You'll Always Find in a Greta Boris Novel*, and *Things You'll Never Find in a Greta Boris Novel*. These are the promises she's making to her readers.

Not only was this a helpful writing exercise, she thinks readers are more interested in what's in it for them than they are in her home life, pets, or writing pedigree. It gives them a quick insight into Greta's books so that they can tell right away if there are any "deal-breakers" that would ruin their enjoyment of the story.

This exercise can also help you further refine your author strategy. Like so many things in this business, crafting a mission statement is a cyclical process. We periodically revisit and refine our own statements as we come to better understand ourselves and our stories.

Action Plan:

1. Using our formula above, write at least three different versions of your author mission statement.
2. Using Greta's format or your own, expand the mission statement into an ABOUT PAGE that

focuses on your promise to the reader. Consider posting this to your own website or working it into your author bio!

Time for the Tagline

A tagline is an elevator pitch for your writing career. In a single, catchy phrase, you're telling your listener what you write.

The idea is to take all the elements, genre, tropes, setting and impact and bake them into a cake with just the right flavor. What you don't want is to call out any one ingredient to the exclusion of the others. A flour cake sounds blah. A sugar cake, too sweet. But an angel food cake sounds great even if we don't know exactly what the ingredients are. Don't give your readers the recipe. Give them a bite.

The mission statement is a great place to start. Completing the action steps in this section should yield a list of words and phrases. This list describes your writing style and purpose.

Filter through these ideas. Which have the most emotional impact? Which have a double or triple meaning that all apply to your writing?

For instance, Megan's tagline is: Escape into Myth, Magic, and Mayhem

Escape is an emotive word. It shows the entertainment value of her stories. She wants readers to feel transported out of their everyday lives into someplace extraordinary.

Another key to writing a good tagline is to find words that can do more than one job. *Escape* does that for Megan. Along with having an emotional impact, it also tells us something about the type of story readers can expect. Megan's protagonists are on a journey. Her books are portal fantasy. The characters move between realms.

If the genre is in doubt, *Myth* and *Magic* take care of that.

They identify the books as fantasies. They also call out two important tropes in her stories. In Chapter 19, we mentioned Megan uses myths from other cultures as jumping-off places in her work. And, of course, magic is key in fantasy.

Finally, *Mayhem* implies an action-packed adventure. It tells you these stories won't be all sunshine and lollipops. You're more likely to run into a carnivorous pixie than a bunny rabbit.

Greta's tagline is: Murders that Hit Home

Murders is pretty straightforward. It lets people know there will be crime. There will be dead bodies. *Hit Home* is the hard-working phrase. It does several jobs.

First, it gives readers more information about the subgenres Greta writes in. Her stories are domestic mysteries, not global thrillers. The protagonists aren't FBI agents or police detectives or navy seals. The books take place in homes, beauty salons, Pilates studios and even mortuaries. In fact, Greta lives in Southern California and sets her books there.

Hit Home also implies that the stories will make the reader think about themselves and their lives and maybe make them laugh. In other words, they're thoughtful and maybe humorous.

We suggest you pull apart your mission statement. Make lists of words or phrases that suggest the genre, settings, themes, and so on. Use a thesaurus to find alliterative, punchy, or unusual words, then play with them. Try out different combinations, synonyms, and so on.

Once you have five or ten, it's time to test them out.

We all need feedback on our writing. Whether it's our novel, back cover book descriptions, or our taglines, good constructive criticism helps us refine and improve our work. Don't skip this step.

Send the taglines out into the world. You can email them to writer friends, post them on Facebook groups, send them to your readers, or even ask strangers.

See which people like best. Sit and listen. Don't explain or interrupt, but compare their reactions with what you were trying to express. Do their responses match your mission statement? If so, great! If not, it's time to try again.

Don't be surprised if you go through multiple iterations of this exercise. Be patient and give yourself time. Once you find a tagline that sings for you, put it on your website, your social media pages, or print it on a t-shirt. Your readers will love it.

If you'd like to break the mission statement and tagline creation process down into step-by-step daily practice, we recommend grabbing our free email mini-course Getting to the Heart of Your Author Brand—a seven day mini-course at www.AuthorWheel.com/Foundations.

Action Plan:

1. Spend at least 5-10 minutes to compile a complete list of all the words you can think of from the previous three chapters. Don't edit or judge.
2. Using that list of words, write at least ten possible taglines for your writing.

Chapter 21
Assessing Your Strengths
& Facing Your
Weaknesses

Once you have a mission statement and tagline, you should have a pretty good idea of what you write and why. You should know what you're trying to accomplish and have a general sense of the kinds of readers you're trying to reach with your books.

You have a compass. These two statements will help guide your writing choices. Now you need a map.

You can't plot your journey to a successful author career—as you define it—until you know where you're starting from. Our journey begins by understanding our strengths and weaknesses, so that we'll be prepared for the twists, turns, and forks in the road.

This chapter might be difficult to get through. Self-assessment isn't easy. But it's important.

We'll start with our strengths, which hopefully feels a little more comfortable.

Understanding Your Strengths

What are you good at? What have you learned in school or other jobs that might give you an advantage in the writing and publishing world?

In business circles, we often call our strengths a "competitive advantage." These are the things that make our products stand out or our businesses more profitable. For authors, it's what makes our stories unique, our books appealing to readers, and our marketing effective.

Megan loves learning. She spends a lot of time reading and exploring a wide range of subjects directly and indirectly related to her fiction. This includes hundreds of hours of courses and dozens of books on writing craft and the publishing industry. She also digs deep to learn as much as she can about the myths and legends that make up her fictional worlds.

Her writing benefits from her research skills. Multiple reviews have mentioned the strength of her worldbuilding. It's also reflected in the quality of her books. Even in the early days of self-publishing she received compliments that her books were indistinguishable from her traditionally published counterparts.

So research is one of Megan's strengths. However, she also has experience as a manager in the corporate world. This is the foundation of her ability to organize and manage her publishing projects. She understands how to create and execute a project plan.

Greta has been a teacher and a trainer for much of her adult life. One of her strengths is communication and another is understanding human nature. Both assets influence her fiction writing. Readers regularly mention that her characters feel genuine, like people you might know. And, of course, good communication is fundamental to writing.

Action Plan:

Set aside time to think through the things you're good at. Consider the following:

1. Education—What classes have you taken that would benefit a writing career?
2. Past Work Experience—How might it be applicable to writing and publishing?
3. Hobbies—Art hobbies lend themselves to graphic design work. Sports hobbies teach leadership and teamwork. Or maybe they become the subject matter of your books.
4. Personality—What is it about you as a person that sets you apart from others?
5. Home Life—Do you have kids at home? A stable job you love? A supportive spouse? What about your home life will help you succeed?
6. Financial—What kind of financial investment can you make in your career? (This could be a strength or a weakness.)

Brainstorm or journal your thoughts in a notebook. Give yourself time and space to think deeply about your strengths so you can lean into those skills in the future.

Facing Your Weaknesses

Now that you know what you're good at, it's time to face the things that are hard.

We all have things that we struggle with. It's a simple fact of life. We can't be good at everything, and the world would be pretty boring if we were.

Weaknesses don't have to be entirely negative, however. Once you recognize them, you can find ways to overcome them, or even use them to your advantage. In fact, creativity often thrives when presented with constraints.

Think about a time you were in school and had to write an essay. If the teacher didn't give you a topic to write about, did you struggle to get started? What if the teacher asked you to write an essay on what you did last summer? So much easier, right?

Creating an effective author career strategy is similar. By understanding our weaknesses (constraints) we're pushed to find creative solutions that can usher in the success we're looking for.

When Megan started writing what would become her first published novel, she had a three month old baby at home. Her time was not fully her own. Worse, she couldn't create a fixed schedule. The baby slept when she slept, and that was the only time Megan had to work on the story.

On one hand, this was a weakness. Megan couldn't predictably work during the day, or even during her most creative hours. Instead, she had to learn how to be flexible around her baby's sleep time and make the most of every minute the house was quiet. That flexibility still serves her today.

Greta isn't a "math" person. She doesn't do spreadsheets. However, if you're running a business, you've got to buck up and figure out your ROI on things like ads and independent contractor costs.

Rather than fail financially, she sought out people who can help her. She has Megan (who loves spreadsheets) at The Author Wheel, and she's purchased online courses that come with built-in spreadsheets on the fiction side of things. The people and courses she's aligned herself with, have given her much more than math.

What do you struggle with? What are your constraints?

Action Plan:

Set aside some time to think through your weaknesses and constraints. Consider:

1. Time Management—What's your schedule like? If necessary, review the section on Productive Writing Habits.
2. Current Job—This relates to time management, but what demands does your current job make on your time and ability to write? Is this something you love, or dislike?
3. Missing Skills—What skills necessary for writing and publishing are you lacking? Common ones are graphic design and advertising.
4. Personality—Are you an introvert who hates crowds and struggles to engage with readers? Are you an Enneagram Individualist who feels like a sellout for asking people to pay for your writing?
5. Financial—What kind of financial investment can you make in your career? (This could be a strength or a weakness.)
6. Home Life—This is a tough one, but consider how your personal situation might affect your writing and publishing goals.

Brainstorm or journal your thoughts in a notebook. Give yourself time and space to think deeply about your weaknesses so you can find creative solutions to those constraints.

Chapter 22
Mapping a Path

There are several things to think about when you're developing your author career strategy. Your strengths and weaknesses are first so you know where you're starting from, but you also need a destination.

As mentioned in the last chapter, the mission statement and tagline are your compass. Your self-assessment is your origin. The next step is to target a destination.

This is not goal setting. Not yet. This is a vision for your future, a broad sense of what it will take for you to feel successful.

Creating a Vision

This part of the Author Career Strategy is very personal. Every author will have a different definition of success. Your ideal life will differ from ours and the other authors in your writing group.

To get started, grab your journal and close your eyes. Imagine yourself in the life you want. What does your day look like when you're a successful author?

Use all your senses. Give yourself some time to feel what

that success is like. What do you hear? What do you smell? Where are you? Who's with you?

After you've spent some time visualizing your future, open your journal and answer the following questions:

1. How do you define author success?
2. What kind of lifestyle do you dream of having in the future?
3. Where do you want to be geographically?
4. How will you engage with your readers? Where are they in the world?
5. How do you want to run your business? Will you remain a solo operator, or will you have a team of assistants? Will you publish through traditional presses, indie publish, or both? (There's more on traditional vs. indie in the next chapter.)
6. Do you want to travel on big book tours, or live a quiet life at home?

Use these questions to get you started, but don't limit yourself to these alone. Write anything that comes to mind related to your ideal future life. Take as long as you need.

We're writers, so writing these things down often makes sense, but some people prefer creating vision boards. If that sounds fun and interesting to you, here are a few options to consider.

- Grab some old magazines and find inspirational pictures and quotes. Cut and paste your favorites to a posterboard you can hang on your office wall to look at every day.
- Collect inspirational items and create a "future memory" box with an old shoe box

- Create a diorama of your perfect day
- If you're more digital minded, start a vision board on Pinterest or in Trello. You could also use presentation software like Keynote, PowerPoint, or Google Slides to collect your ideas and dreams.

Whatever inspires you and helps you envision success will work. Spend enough time to feel you have a solid grasp of your dream, but not so much that it's keeping you away from actually writing. That's definitely not our goal.

Remember, you can always add to or edit your vision board. Like your mission statement, tagline, or any other part of the author strategy process, these are living documents. They're bound to change. That's okay. Good, even. You'll want to revisit them every few months to reassess and motivate yourself to keep going, especially when times are tough.

Action Plan:

1. Journal your thoughts and create a vision board in whatever way makes the most sense to you.
2. Go back and look at your mission statement and tagline...do they fit with this future? If not, what needs to change about them to bring them into alignment?

Leaning Into Your Strengths

With your vision in mind, go back to the list of strengths you created in Chapter 21. Consider which of these strengths can help you on your journey toward the future.

For example, if you see yourself as an indie author entrepreneur and you have a background in graphic design, guess what? You can use your skills to create images for marketing and building your business. Not only will you be able to create a brand that fully represents you and your work, but you'll save money that can be spent on other things.

Or maybe you're a strong team leader and good at organizing people and projects. Building a team and delegating tasks will help you accomplish all your goals more quickly. If you're an extrovert who loves being around people and talking about your books, live events should be part of your plans. Writers with strong technical or computer skills can build their own websites. You get the idea.

Many of these skills can be learned, of course, but capitalizing on the skills you already have provides a great foundation for success.

Action Plan:

1. Return to Chapter 21 and pick out at least 5-10 skills or strengths that will help you on your journey toward your vision of success.
2. For each of the selected skills, write 1-3 ways you can use that skill in your author career.

Overcoming Your Weaknesses/Challenges,

Weaknesses don't make you weak. In fact, we like to think of them merely as constraints. They are the boundaries within which you have to work, or the obstacles that require creative solutions to circumvent.

As mentioned earlier, one of Megan's early challenges was finding the time to write with a newborn at home. We should also add that the child in question did not like to be put down for naps. She wanted to be held or feel someone close while she slept. As a result, Megan's time was limited and unpredictable. That was her constraint.

Her solution was to strap the baby into a wrap or carrier so that she could hold her daughter, hands free. Then, when the baby was comfy and cozy, she would stand at the kitchen island swaying side-to-side while typing on her computer. The baby got a nap, and Megan got some words on the page.

Was it a perfect solution? No. But Megan made progress.

Another potential weakness that could affect your career strategy is writing speed. If you're a fast writer who can draft a story in a matter of weeks, that's a great strength. But if the draft is messy and you hate editing, you'll have to find help to polish your story before publishing.

If you're a slower writer, your draft might be less error-prone, but it will probably take you longer to publish each book. You may need to study ways to increase your writing speed, or consider which publishing strategies work better for slower releases.

Action Plan:

1. Return to Chapter 21 and pick out at least 5-10 weaknesses or constraints that could become obstacles in your journey toward success.
2. For each of the selected weaknesses, write 1-3 ways you can work around or overcome that obstacle.

Common Strategies to Consider

We can't list all author career strategies in this section, but here are a few common ones to get you started. We've also mentioned the strengths and weaknesses that lend themselves to each. Keep in mind, your mileage may vary. You are unique, your vision is unique, and we can't tell you exactly what will work for you.

Consider the following basic strategies carefully. If any seem appealing, investigate further. Test out some tactics mentioned and see how they feel. (We'll talk more about tactics in Chapter 23.) If you don't find a fit, drop it. Move on to the next in the list.

Traditional Publishing

Broadly speaking, there are two primary book publishing strategies: Traditional, where you seek an agent and a contract with a publisher; and Independent (Self) Publishing, where you become your own publisher. These two overarching strategies are like the broad genre categories for your book. Greta writes Mysteries and Megan writes Fantasy. The nuance comes in the details.

There are fewer decisions for the author to make in traditional publishing. If you pursue this path, you're looking for another company to do the heavy lifting of book production for you. They will make most of the high-level marketing decisions (like launch date, cover design, pricing, advertising budget, etc.) but will rely on the author for much of the social media and online promotion.

The two big decisions a traditional author has to make are:

1. Whether to pursue an agent and go for a contract with one of the big publishers, or seek a smaller press that doesn't require an agent; and,
2. What they want to write for their next project.

Sometimes the former dictates the latter. For example, if you get a publishing deal for the first book in a projected trilogy, your next two projects have already been decided. You're going to have to finish that trilogy on the publisher's timeline.

Of course, it's always your decision which contracts to sign. If there are terms you don't like, a smaller press might negotiate. The big publishers will probably give you a boiler-plate contract and tell you to take it or leave it, but ultimately, it's still your decision. You decide what's right for your author career.

Independent (Self) Publishing

Indie authors are no longer looked down on as much as they once were. Some in academic or literary communities still snub them, but readers rarely pay attention to how a book was published as long as the story is good and it comes in a pretty package.

The independent publishing strategy requires a broader set of skills. The author becomes the publisher. You wear both the creative hat and the business hat in this scenario, and switching hats can be challenging. However, the rewards often outweigh the risks. You'll earn more money per book and have full control over the production and sales decisions for that title.

Our book PUBLISH: *Take Charge of Your Author Career,* and the companion course, *Self-Publish or Get an Agent,* cover the various publishing paths. We go into detail about how each works, the pros and cons, and we give you action steps to get you started on the path you choose.

In this book, we're going to assume you know the basics of traditional vs. independent publishing. In fact, we're going to assume you've already made your choice between those two. The rest of the strategies listed are more nuanced or niche publishing strategies. Most are decisions that the independent authors will have to face, but some apply to traditional authors as well.

Rapid Release

If you're naturally a fast writer, publishing quickly can do amazing things for your sales momentum. Having preorders up for Books 2 & 3 when you release Book 1 can boost sales. Fast readers like to binge an entire series in a matter of days or weeks.

This strategy works fabulously for popular fiction genres like Romance, Science-Fiction, Fantasy, or Thrillers.

A variation on this strategy is to "hold back" on releasing the first few titles in a new series. Once you have three or four books ready, you can begin launching them within three to five weeks of each other as you continue writing new books. The end of the series might take longer to release, but by then you've captured the attention of the binge readers.

The downside of the rapid release strategy can be a high level of burnout. If you're naturally a slower writer, attempting to keep up this pace might leave you exhausted and creatively blocked. Or even physically injured.

If you're a fast writer and rapid release sounds interesting, you can learn more in the 20 Books to 50k Facebook group.

Kindle Unlimited

Kindle Unlimited (KU) is Amazon's monthly book-membership club. Readers pay a monthly fee to borrow as many titles as they want. Amazon compensates authors for the number of pages read each month, rather than the number of books downloaded. However, ebooks enrolled in KU can't be sold anywhere else.

Selling books exclusively through Amazon is appealing to many authors. It allows them better visibility on the largest, most popular online bookstore in the world, and makes it easier to manage their titles. They don't have to upload their books across multiple bookstores and track sales across platforms.

Greta put her newest series in KU as a short-term strategy while she learns how to indie publish. This allows her to take things one step at a time. She can learn the basics and build her readership without becoming mired in the technical aspects of all the different bookstores.

KU is a strategy that lends itself well to authors who can also follow the Rapid Release model. Kindle Unlimited rewards new releases with better visibility, and people in KU tend to be voracious readers. If you have a long series, a big backlist, or can be ready with the next book on preorder, you can really do well through the KU program.

However, authors who write books more slowly might find their visibility drops off between releases. And because of KU's exclusivity requirement, they're forced to rely on that single income stream.

(Side note: paperbacks are not included in the program and do not have to be sold exclusively on Amazon.)

For some authors, including Megan, it doesn't feel right to rely on a single platform. Amazon could change its rules or payment structure at any moment. If they did, and if it negatively affected her income and her ability to reach readers, she'd be out of luck. However, there are a lot of "what-ifs" embedded in those statements. For many—arguably most—authors, the benefits of KU outweigh the risks.

For more information on the Kindle Unlimited program from authors, visit Amazon's Author Central platform.

Selling Wide

One of the biggest rules in personal finance is to diversify your assets. Megan studied finance in college and worked at a private investment firm for several years, so this rule has been ingrained in her psyche. For her, the idea of being exclusive with Amazon feels risky. She doesn't want to be reliant on a single platform for all her book sales, nor give them control over her access to readers.

Instead, she's chosen to "go wide" and sell ebooks across as many retailers as possible. This includes Amazon (but not Kindle Unlimited), Barnes & Noble, Apple Books, Google Play, Kobo, and more.

It's more work to set up. You must upload your book to each platform and maintain records of everything. It also takes longer to build your audience. However, most of the non-Amazon platforms reward longevity. More in-tune with traditional publishers, they don't expect authors to release a new book every month.

There are also services that will take your book files and distribute them to all the different platforms for you. Draft2Digital and Publish Drive are two of the more popular of these "aggregators."

Most traditional publishers sell widely. If you're a traditionally published author, you likely won't get a choice in the matter.

For specific tactics to use with each of the major platforms and more up-to-date advice on selling wide, check out the Wide for the Win Facebook group.

Direct Sales

Direct sales occur when an author sells books without the help of a store. They can do this in several ways and in combination with other strategies to reach readers.

For example, live events like book fairs and conventions can be a great direct-sale tactic. Authors can meet existing fans, find new readers, and sell books—especially paperback books. Even non-book events can be excellent opportunities. We know authors who have built their careers on getting booths at home shows or craft fairs.

Another way to sell direct is through your own author website. Ecommerce platforms like Shopify can help you build an online book business. If you're in KU, you can sell signed paperbacks on your own site, or set up drop shipping directly to customers. If you're wide, you can also sell ebooks and audiobooks by integrating your website with BookFunnel, a fabulous ebook distributor.

Direct Sales work well for authors who are tech savvy (for online sales) or enjoy going to in-person events. If you have a background in sales, this could be a brilliant strategy for you. However, for authors who have little computer experience or who are extremely introverted, the Direct Sales model might not be a good fit.

For more information on Selling Direct, we recommend picking up *Get Your Book Selling Direct,* by Monica Leonelle and Russell Nohelty.

Business Around Your Book

If you're a non-fiction author, this strategy might be perfect for you. Many non-fiction authors are less interested in making an income purely from book sales. Sure, it would be lovely, but really they wrote the book to help existing clients or to attract new ones. The book is a tool for bigger sales.

Greta's very first book was actually a non-fiction nutrition and fitness guide written for her personal training clients. At the time, she was a personal trainer and wellness coach. She used the book as a calling card, or proof of her expertise, more than as a money-maker. Many professional speakers have a book to support their career.

Side Hustle

Do you love your day job? Not every author has a goal of going full time. In fact, some of our author friends feel like they write more and write better when they have the time constraints a day job provides. A regular paycheck and health benefits can minimize the pressure.

If this sounds like you, lean into it! You don't have to rapid release or worry about being a bestseller or launching each book to huge numbers. Maintaining this mindset could be incredibly freeing. Sure, you want to find readers and you want your books to be successful, but if you remove yourself from the rat race, you might find the entire process is more joyful.

With this strategy, it becomes critical to focus only on the essential elements of your business. Dedicated writing time, project planning for your book launch, and targeted reader outreach will be key. As much as possible, avoid "shiny thing syndrome" and don't follow the crowd. You're already mapping your own path. Don't blindly follow someone else or you might end up in quicksand.

Retirement Gig

We have had many students in our courses who began writing after retirement. Their kids were out of the house. The day job no longer consumed them. They'd always wanted to write a book but never found the time. Now they were ready.

Retired writers—assuming they retired voluntarily with savings in the bank—have a leg up on the rest of us. They're often looking for a bit of supplemental income, but most want to fill their time with an activity that they love. If this sounds like you, make the most of it.

The retirement-gig strategy means you can choose how to structure your days. You can try on a lot of different hats, see what fits, and return the rest. If you don't want to learn how to advertise on Facebook, don't. If you want to experiment with short stories, go for it.

That said, if you want readers to buy your book and give you that steady bit of supplemental income, you need to treat your writing as a business. Don't flinch away from hiring a good cover designer—unless you're a graphic designer by trade. Readers can tell. Similarly, you'll need to find professional editors.

Always keep your mission statement and tagline in mind. As with all of these strategies, focusing on your core values and purpose will keep you on the path to your version of success.

A warning for the Retirement-Gig writers out there: Vanity presses love to prey on your insecurities. If a company is asking you to pay them to publish your book, be very wary. Always check <u>Writer Beware</u> before signing with anyone. Read contracts carefully so you'll understand what you're paying for and what you're giving away. If a contract says the publisher will own your copyright after you've paid them to publish the book, walk away.

Action Plan:

1. Decide if you want to pursue an agent and a traditional publishing deal, or go the "indie" route and be your own publisher
2. Review each of the strategies listed above. For any that sound interesting, compare your skills and

weaknesses to the description. What do you do well that would lend itself to that strategy? What constraints will you have to overcome to be successful?

3. Follow the links to learn more about the strategies that seem most interesting to you.

Chapter 23
Implementing Tactics and Setting Goals

N
ow that you've decided on the author strategies you plan to use, it's time to choose your tactics, and set goals to implement them.

But first, what's the difference between a strategy and a tactic?

Strategy is the overarching plan. Tactics are lists of tasks or activities that will implement your strategy. Tasks are the individual action items on your to-do list.

For example:

- If you've decided to sell direct, one tactic would be selling in-person at comic conventions. A task that fulfills that tactic would be to apply for a booth at your local comic convention.
- If you chose a wide sales strategy, a tactic would be to apply for promotions at various retailers each month. A task in that tactic would be to research available promotions at Barnes and Noble.

- If you chose to put your books in Kindle Unlimited, a tactic would be to run a Countdown Deal. A task would be to schedule that Countdown Deal.

Each of these tactics are actions taken to pursue the bigger strategy. Each task is the smallest possible to-do item that can be added to your preferred daily or weekly planner.

Taking our direct sales example, to sell at in-person comic conventions you'd need to:

- Research and make a list of conventions you'd like to attend.
- Visit each website and find the application criteria and cost to have a booth at the event.
- Fill out the application form and submit it.
- Order banners and decor for your table.
- Create a budget for your events.
- Buy books so you have enough inventory to sell.

This list could keep going, but you get the idea. The smaller you can make those tasks, the easier each one will be to complete.

The good news is that the more tasks you complete, the more motivation you'll have to keep going. Each time you check an item off your list, a little dopamine is released into your system. We teach this in our Finish Your Book Faster course. It's how we gamify our writing, and you can use it to gamify your general productivity as well.

Action Plan:

1. In your journal, write 5-10 tactics you'd like to try implementing for your chosen strategy. Prioritize

them from the most impactful and interesting to the least impactful and interesting.

2. For your highest priority tactic, write all the individual tasks you will need to complete to implement that tactic. Each task should be one step and have its own line.

3. Repeat for the top 3-5 tactics you'd like to implement this year.

Planning Your Year

You've decided on a strategy. You've thought through the tactics you'll implement to make it happen. You've created a list of tasks. Now it's time to set your goals and put everything on the calendar.

Similar to the goal-setting chapter in the Productive Writing Habits section of this book, we like to use the SMART goal setting method. Now, we're going to apply that to our overall career, and chart our path for the next ten years.

Sound overwhelming? Don't worry, we're going to walk you through it.

Let's start with a reminder of the SMART framework.

S - Specific
M - Measurable
A - Attainable
R - Realistic
T - Time-Bound

Goals must be specific, or we have no idea if we've achieved them. An example of a specific goal might be to learn to use Facebook ads to market books.

To make this goal measurable, you might say you want to learn to double your current monthly income using Facebook ads to market your books.

To make it attainable, for us at least, this would include purchasing a book or a course. Facebook ads are a complicated and potentially expensive marketing medium. It would be better to learn from someone who's an expert than to try to figure it out alone.

Realistically, you discover you will probably need a budget of $200 to $300 dollars to test ads and figure out the profit-making process. You also learn it will take you two to three months.

Finally, you put this whole thing on the calendar, making it time bound. You set a start and end date for taking a class or reading a book, then a start date for your first ad campaign.

That's the SMART goal-setting method in a nutshell, but the time bound piece of the puzzle is often elusive. How long does it take to build a mailing list? Master Facebook ads? Write three more novels in our series?

Most people underestimate what they can accomplish in the long term, and overestimate what they can accomplish in the short term. One way to avoid that frustration is to start with the long range goal and divide it into smaller and smaller pieces.

Dream Big, Work Backward

Let's revisit the Big Dream you journaled about in Chapter 18. After the work you've done so far, does this Big Dream still fit in your vision of the future?

If we've done our jobs correctly, your Big Dream should align with your author mission statement, author tagline, and chosen career strategy. What if the dream isn't compatible with the strategy? Say you envisioned a publisher-sponsored book tour. However, you're now interested in independent publishing via Kindle Unlimited. Obviously, you need to reassess.

If you're still in alignment, it's time to flesh out your Big Dream and make it a ten-year goal.

Ten years is a long time. Therefore, the ten-year goal can be huge. Do you want to be a six-figure author who's invited to speak at indie author conventions? Will your publisher send you on a national book tour, where you'll sign books at stores across the country? Will you have a line of readers eagerly waiting to meet you? How many books are in your backlist? Will you have a movie deal?

Don't underestimate yourself. You can accomplish great things in a decade. Your life could completely change. Imagine that future.

Next, think about the five-year plan. If in the ten-year dream included a twenty book backlist, then in five years you should have ten. If you said you want to have a big publisher sponsoring your national book tour, first you'll need a publisher. What can you accomplish in five years? It's still a lot.

Now take it a little smaller. What can you do in three years that will move you toward your Big Dream? Smaller still, what can you accomplish in the next twelve months? What about the next three months? What are your priorities for this month? This week?

An Example:

Let's say you've decided you want to use the Direct Sales strategy to sell books from your own website. You already have your site set up and books ready to sell, but your mailing list is small. To achieve your ten-year dream of a six-figure income from direct sales, you need to grow your audience and get them to subscribe to your newsletter.

Looking back on your career, you see it took three years to achieve the number of subscribers you currently have. Although it's likely you could double that number more quickly, it would be safe to give yourself another three years.

Three years is an unwieldy amount of time, however. It's hard to get organized or stay motivated for a three-year project. So, you divide the number of subscribers you hope to gain by three, then make the new number your annual goal. It instantly feels more doable.

There are several tactics you could use to increase your subscriber base. In the first year of your three-year project, you settle on the tactic of writing a novella to attract new readers. You know the novella should be a prequel for your series, and should fulfill the promise of your author tagline. You plan to give the novella away for free as a gift to new subscribers (this is called a lead magnet). Another option is to cross-promote the novella with authors in your genre who have comparable titles to your series.

Here are just some tasks involved with that tactic:

1. Write the novella
2. Edit the novella
3. Format the novella
4. Hire a cover designer
5. Set up a Bookfunnel account and create a landing page for your novella
6. Create a pop-up box and subscribe page on your website with a link to the Bookfunnel landing page
7. Create a welcome sequence in your email provider to welcome those who sign up for your free novella
8. Add a link to the novella's landing page at the end of all your books

9. Submit the novella to author cross-promotions on BookFunnel to reach new readers
10. Research comparable authors in your genre
11. Find out where those comparable authors (and their readers) hang out online
12. Politely ask the comparable authors if they'd be willing to share your free novella with their audience

And so on . . .

It's a lot, and it's going to take time. That's why we suggest breaking your annual goals into quarterly and monthly goals. The first quarter's goal may simply be to create the product, or steps one through three above. You could write this in your journal as:

I will write, edit, and format a prequel novella for my series in the first quarter of this year.

Write the due date on your calendar.

Next, what can you achieve this month? Can you finish the first draft? Write it down:

I will write the first draft of a prequel novella for my series this month. Put the due date on your calendar.

What can you achieve this week?

I will write five thousand words of the first draft of a prequel novella for my series this week.

There you go. Planning 101.

You'll have to repeat this process for each tactic and revisit your goals each week, month, quarter, and year. If you get a little off-track, you can adjust your expectations. For example, if you don't make your subscriber goal in year one, but the pieces are in place, you'll most likely hit your numbers in future years.

If you work faster than expected, you can always start working on the next task on the list. If you've written them in your calendar, you know exactly what you need to do next.

Common Tactics to Consider

Write a Lead Magnet

This can be a full-length novel, novella, or short story to give to readers when they join your mailing list. You can share this in cross-promotions with other authors. Run it in group promotions on sites like BookFunnel. You can also use it as a pop-up on your website, and as a link in the back of your other books. This works well whether you're published traditionally, independently, or selling direct. It's also an excellent strategy for those who're building a business around their nonfiction work.

Build an Author Website

It's a good idea for most authors to have a "home" online where readers can find them. A website can be as simple as a landing page with your bio and list of your titles, or as complicated as an eCommerce site where you sell your own books. Some publishers will create a website for their authors (or give each author their own page) but others will encourage writers to have their own site.

Build a Newsletter Mailing List

Your mailing list is the group of readers who are interested in your work and want to follow your writing progress. You can entice them to sign up for your list with a lead magnet, offer that lead magnet on your own website, as well as cross-promote the magnet with other authors. However, if you want to keep your readers engaged (and remembering who you are and what you write), you'll need to email your list regularly. Most authors send a newsletter monthly, bi-weekly, or weekly.

Author Cross-Promotions

This is a tactic in which you and another comparable author share each other's books with your audiences. You can do this to increase sales. For example, when you run a discount on a book. Or you can share one another's lead magnets to encourage readers to subscribe to your lists. There are also companies that run group promotions. We love BookFunnel for this.

Engage with Readers on Social Media

It's a good idea to be somewhere online where readers can find you. Choose TikTok, Facebook, Instagram, LinkedIn, or any social media platform you're comfortable with. With this tactic, you can choose the type of content you want to share and when you want to share it. This can be a good way to engage directly with readers.

Participate in Live Events

Live events can be a wonderful opportunity to meet readers and talk about books. To find them, consider checking with your local library, online and in-person conventions and conferences. Apply for a table or to be on a panel. If you aren't too introverted to speak in public, this is a great tactic.

Advertise

Advertising is where you pay another company to share your book with their readers. This can be on a social media platform like Facebook, at a retailer like Amazon, or on a book specific mailing list like BookBub. Advertising works well for independent authors, but it carries a financial risk. There's a steep learning curve and not everyone earns a positive return on their investment. This is a more advanced tactic and works best for authors who have at least a few books published.

Implementing Tactics

The more decisions you have to make in a day, the less you'll accomplish. it's simple math. If you have five working hours and you spend one of them figuring out exactly what you need to get done, you now only have four hours to do it.

We've found it's much more efficient to plan things in advance.

For instance, Greta has a goal of sending two newsletters a month to her mailing list. She used to plan that content the week she needed to email. She'd write about something that was on her mind or something that was happening in her writing life. This was fine until it wasn't.

When she ran into some difficult family issues, all her

inspiration dried up. Consequently, she didn't send a newsletter for almost two months. When she finally sent one, she had a flurry of unsubscribes. Some of her subscribers had forgotten who she was.

Now, Greta takes some time once every three months to plot out newsletter ideas for the quarter. She can then put those ideas into her calendar, blocking out the time on the necessary days to write and schedule those emails.

If she's not feeling inspired, it doesn't matter. She knows what she needs to write. She can always change ideas if something more interesting comes up, but if it doesn't, she has a game plan.

When goal setting and implementation planning are done well, our stress levels go down and our productivity goes up. So why don't we do it even when we know we should?

Often, it's because we're unconvinced that the tactics we've chosen are the right ones. We feel we're locking ourselves into a process that might not work. We'd rather wing it for a while until we're certain we're on the right track.

Winging it has its own set of problems. As mentioned, it's stressful, often unproductive, always more inefficient, and it's easy to miss important steps.

Sometimes we feel like planning things out takes too much time away from getting things done. We want to get to work already. Except, when we start without a plan, it's easy to get distracted by mundane tasks. We might feel busy, even if we aren't actually moving toward our goals.

Which is why we suggest building in time to plan and prepare so you're ready to reach your author goals.

Action Plan:

1. Review your Big Dream and make sure it aligns with your author mission statement, tagline, and strategy.
2. Spend 5-10 minutes condensing that Big Dream into a ten-year goal. Write it in your journal.
3. Write SMART goals:

   - A five-year goal
   - A three-year goal
   - A one-year goal
   - This quarter's goal
   - This month's goal
   - Add this week's tasks to your to-do list

If you'd like an easy-to-follow worksheet to bring this all together, visit www.authorwheel.com/foundations to download the free Author Strategy Worksheet.

Chapter 24
Reassessing Things

U nfortunately, not every tactic you try is going to work for you and your books. You may discover you absolutely hate running Facebook ads and struggle to make them profitable. You may discover that taking your books wide takes too much effort, and you liked life better when all your stories were in Kindle Unlimited. If indie publishing sends you into panic attacks, you might decide to try pitching agents. Much of the author biz comes down to trial and error.

Having said all that, if you don't give things a reasonable amount of time to work, you may never know if a tactic is viable or not. Different tactics have different learning curves and growth rates.

Jumping from strategy to strategy and tactic to tactic is a sure-fire way to waste time and money and never see success. However, you can also fall prey to the sunk-cost fallacy. This term describes our tendency to continue doing something that isn't bringing us a benefit. Why? Because we've invested so much time and money into the endeavor, we don't want to give up on it. Both extremes are dangerous.

To avoid both ends of the spectrum, we need to commit to

things for a reasonable timeframe and pick a date and method to reassess. But what's a reasonable timeframe?

Learn from others.

It pays to learn as much as you can from people who are successful at what you want to do. If you're thinking of using direct sales as your primary strategy, find an author who's doing it well. If they write in your genre, so much the better. Learn as much as you can from them.

Find out how big her mailing list is, how long it took her to make the income you'd like to make, and the specific tactics she used to do it. It may seem impossible to get that kind of data, but you'd be surprised how transparent and generous many authors are.

Look for podcasts where authors talk about their publishing journeys. Read industry how-to books that don't make ridiculous promises but give you actual action plans. Talk to writers at conferences, guilds, and organizations. We've put recommendations in the resources section of this book to get you started.

Even though every author's journey is unique, watching how someone else did something you want to do is just common sense. Once you have that information, you'll be able to come up with some tentative timeframes for what you're hoping to accomplish.

Stay the course.

Once you've decided to give a tactic a certain amount of time, don't quit until that period is up unless something catastrophic happens. Disappointments, ups and downs, and rude awakenings are all a part of the process of doing anything worthwhile.

Read up on any famous author, and you'll find out how many times agents or publishers rejected them before they got a contract. You'll also find out how many flops they wrote before they wrote a breakout book. You may even find they wrote in a completely different genre than the one they're known for.

Greta would have given up on the whole writing gig if she hadn't signed a contract for *The Seven Deadly Sins Murders*. She was disappointed with her early book launches and didn't understand that it can take a long time to build a readership. Thankfully, she'd committed to seven books. By the time the last couple were being published, she had a decent sized mailing list and hit the USA Today list in an anthology.

Gather data and reassess.

Once the time or process you committed to is up, gather data and reevaluate. As we stated before, blindly continuing a losing venture is just as detrimental to your success as not giving things enough time.

Fiction authors deal in emotions. We write struggling characters and strive to tug on the heartstrings of readers. But when it comes to the business side of the writing life, we have to put feelings aside and look at the facts.

If you committed to learning how to run Facebook ads for three months, and you've done all the things you set out to do, but the ads still aren't turning a profit, it's probably time to try something else.

Thankfully, there are many paths to success in this business. If one thing isn't working, there are lots more to try. Every turn of the author wheel brings new opportunities.

Part Five
Closing Thoughts

Chapter 25
Authors' Note

This omnibus of quick guides was created to give you a solid foundation on which to build your writing career. There is a lot to learn. We've found when teaching in-person courses that often our newer students are overwhelmed. They don't know what they don't know. It's impossible to make good decisions when you aren't aware of the choices available.

Foundations of Great Storytelling provides a framework to help you sort through all the advice that's swirling around you. There are tons of outstanding books and courses that delve into the details. They explain the three act structure, how to write 10,000 words a day, or how to run Amazon ads. Rather than replicate that work, we've endeavored to show you when, how, and why you might use that information.

Whether you're struggling with time management, understanding where your book fits in the market, or puzzling over standalone or series writing, we've given you tools. When you want to go deep into anything we mention, we've provided additional resources at the end of each section. The books and courses listed are vetted and trusted.

As we've said over and over, success looks different for

every author. Rather than send you down one particular path, *Foundations of Great Storytelling* is designed to give you an overview of what's available in today's shifting publishing world. We hope it brings you clarity and peace so you can keep your stories rolling!

Chapter 26
Resources for Further Learning

Books

Most of the following books are available in our Author Wheel Online Bookstore: https://bookshop.org/shop/authorwheel.

Writing Craft

The Anatomy of a Best Seller, by Sacha Black

The Anatomy of Genre, by John Truby

The Anatomy of Story, by John Truby

How to Write a Series, by Sarah Rosett

Save the Cat Writes a Novel, by Jessica Brody

Take Off Your Pants: Outline Your Books for Faster, Better Writing, 2nd Edition, by Libby Hawker

The Three Story Method, by J. Thorn and Zach Bohannon

The Trope Thesaurus, by Jennifer Hilt

Writing Productivity

The 8-Minute Writing Habit: Create a Consistent Writing Habit that Works with Your Busy Lifestyle, by Monica Leonelle

2,000 to 10,000: How to Write Faster, Write Better, and Write More of What You Love, by Rachel Aaron

5,000 Words Per Hour, by Chris Fox

Dictate Your Book: How to Write Your Book Better, Faster, and Smarter, by Monica Leonelle

Lifelong Writing Habit: The Secret to Writing Every Day, by Chris Fox

The Miracle Morning for Writers: How to Build a Writing Ritual that Increases Your Impact and Your Income (Before 8am), by Hall Elrod and Steve Scott

Write Better Faster: How to Triple Your Writing Speed and Write More Every Day, by Monica Leonelle

Publishing & Business

PUBLISH - Take Charge of Your Author Career, by G.C. Boris and M. Haskell

Get Your Book Selling Direct, by Monica Leonelle and Russell Nohelty

Get Your Book Selling on Kickstarter, by Monica Leonelle and Russell Nohelty

Write to Riches, by Renee Rose

Write to Market: Deliver a Book that Sells, by Chris Fox

Creative Health

The Author Brain: Banish Brain Fog, Beat Writer's Block, Write More Books, by Roland Denzel

Dear Writer, You Need to Quit, by Becca Syme

The Healthy Writer, by Joanna Penn

The Mental Game of Writing, by James Scott Bell

Reclaim Your Author Career: Using the Enneagram to build your strategy, unlock deeper purpose, and celebrate your career, by Claire Taylor

Brainstorming, Worldbuilding, and Research

The Enneagram Institute Website for understanding personality types: https://www.enneagraminstitute.com

Worldbuilding for Fantasy Fans and Authors, by M.D. Presley

Classes:

DIY MFA, by Gabriela Perreira

Finish Your Novel Faster, by The Author Wheel

Getting Serious about Writing a Series, by Lisa Wells

Layering Your Story World: How to Make Fiction Feel Real, by The Author Wheel (Coming Soon!)

Self-Publish or Get an Agent? How to Find and Implement Your Best Path to Publishing Success, by The Author Wheel

Trope-Stacking and Other Genre Magic, by The Author Wheel (Coming Soon!)

Communities

20 Books to 50k - Facebook Group

The Indy Author - www.theindyauthor.com

Wide for the Win - Facebook Group

Podcasts

The Author Wheel Podcast

The Creative Penn Podcast

The Creative Shift with Dan Blank

The Dialogue Doctor

The Indy Author Podcast

I Wish I'd Known Then for Writers

Sell More Books Show

Join The Author Wheel Community!

Visit **www.AuthorWheel.com/Foundations** to join our online community and download the free resources mentioned in this book:

- Know Your Genre Exercise
- Worldbuilding Checklist for Any Genre
- Writing Diary Template
- Author Strategy Template
- Getting to the Heart of Your Author Brand Mini-Course

The Author Wheel Podcast

Don't forget to check out The Author Wheel Podcast. Each week we interview authors and publishing industry leaders about how they overcame their writing roadblocks and found success.

https://authorwheelpodcast.buzzsprout.com

About the Authors

Greta Boris is the USA Today Bestselling author of *The Mortician Murders*, a paranormal suspense series, and *The Seven Deadly Sins Murders*, a psychological suspense series. She hails from sunny So. Cal. where–based on her books which are all set there–things are darker than you'd expect. Her stories have been called atmospheric and un-put-down-able.

To learn more, visit her at www.GretaBoris.com and pick up a free novella while you're there.

* * *

Megan Haskell is the award-winning author of *The Sanyare Chronicles*, an action-packed portal fantasy adventure, and *The Rise of Lilith* series, a contemporary mythological fantasy. A Southern California transplant, she's living the dream of writing while raising her two daughters in Orange County.

Visit her website at www.MeganHaskell.com to learn more and download a free short story.

* * *

Together, Great and Megan founded **The Author Wheel**, which publishes books, courses, and a podcast to help writers overcome their roadblocks and keep their stories rolling. With over twenty years of writing and publishing experience between them, they've made the mistakes so you don't have to.

Visit www.AuthorWheel.com for weekly blog posts on the craft and business of writing.

Also by The Author Wheel

Books

Publish: Take Charge of Your Author Career (Second Edition)

Planning a Novel: How to Activate Your Imagination and Develop a Story You Can Write

Productive Writing Habits: How to Set Goals You'll Keep and Make the Most of Your Writing Time

Understanding Your Genre: How to Write What Readers Want

Courses

Finish Your Novel Faster

Layering Your Story World: How to Make Fiction Feel Real - Coming Soon!

Self-Publish or Get an Agent? How to Find and Implement Your Best Path to Publishing Success

Trope-Stacking and Other Genre Magic - Coming Soon!

Learn more at www.AuthorWheel.com

Also by Greta Boris

The Seven Deadly Sins Murders

The Margin of Lust

The Scent of Wrath

The Sanctity of Sloth

The Color of Envy

A Pinch of Gluttony

The Key of Greed

The Peril of Pride

The Mortician Murders

To Dye For

Hair Today, Gone Tomorrow

Bald-Headed Lies

A Permanent Solution

Buzz Cut

Also by Megan Haskell

The Sanyare Chronicles

The Last Descendant

The Heir Apparent

The Rebel Apprentice

Guardian

The Winter Warrior

The War of the Nine Faerie Realms

Forged in Shadow

Quenched in Secrets - Coming Soon!

The Rise of Lilith Series

Aether Bound

Aether Crossed - Coming Soon!

Notes

7. Brainstorming

1. Wong, M. (2014, April 24). *Stanford study finds walking improves creativity*. Stanford News. Retrieved August 1, 2022, from https://news.stanford.edu/2014/04/24/walking-vs-sitting-042414/

13. Setting S.M.A.R.T. Goals

1. Economy, P. (2018, February 28). *This is the way you need to write down your goals for faster success*. Inc.com. Retrieved February 16, 2022, from https://www.inc.com/peter-economy/this-is-way-you-need-to-write-down-your-goals-for-faster-success.html

16. Writing More Efficiently

1. Csikszentmihalyi, M. (2009). *Flow: The psychology of optimal experience*. Harper and Row.

17. Avoiding Burnout

1. Vlahos, James. "Is Sitting a Lethal Activity?" *The New York Times*, The New York Times, 15 Apr. 2011, https://www.nytimes.com/2011/04/17/magazine/mag-17sitting-t.html.
2. Levine, James A. "The 'NEAT Defect' in Human Obesity: The Role of Nonexercise Activity Thermogenesis." *Mayo Clinic*, Endocrinology Update Volume 2 Number 1, 2007, https://www.mayoclinic.org/documents/mc5810-0307-pdf/DOC-20079082.

www.ingramcontent.com/pod-product-compliance
Lightning Source LLC
Chambersburg PA
CBHW031123020426
42333CB00012B/207